DIFFERENT

THE HIGHLY SENSITIVE
LEADERSHIP REVOLUTION

XO, Heather ♡

HEATHER DOMINICK

Different: The Highly Sensitive Leadership Revolution
Published by EnergyRICH coaching, Inc.
New York, New York

ISBN: 979-8-9868509-0-0
BUSINESS & ECONOMICS / Leadership

Cover and interior design by Victoria Wolf, wolfdesignandmarketing.com.
Copyright owned by Heather Dominick-Kosmicki

A COURSE IN
BUSINESS**MIRACLES**®
HIGHLY SENSITIVE LEADERSHIP

To Karen, I owe you everything.

CONTENTS

PREFACE

I STARTED WRITING THIS BOOK in 2019. I came to the process kicking and screaming, swirling in the all-too-familiar highly sensitive person conundrum of "What's wrong with me?"

What is wrong with me? I wondered. Everyone wants to write a book, yet I'm feeling like a death sentence has been placed on my head. No one is making me do this.

This was only partly true. The true part was that no one was making me; the not-so-true part was that it didn't really feel like a choice, but more like a calling.

I tugged and pulled my way through the writing process over the next twelve months, both loving and loathing the idea of writing a book about how to be successfully self-employed as a person who is highly sensitive.

My reluctance was a mystery to me. I knew that through the process of being self-employed I had personally transformed my life and healed so many of my own *untrained* highly sensitive wounds. I also knew and believed deeply in the way I had helped the highly sensitive entrepreneurs I mentored for nearly a decade do the same.

So, what was the problem?

And then 2019 became 2020, and the reluctance suddenly made sense. As the world was turned upside down in March of that year, with a global pandemic spreading faster than lightning and then racial tensions rising across the United States just a few months later, I realized I wasn't meant to teach only about how to be successfully self-employed as a highly sensitive; I was meant to teach about how to *lead* as a highly sensitive.

Now I understood why I was guided to write a book.

Though it might sound odd, I knew I had been training for the exceptional times of 2020 most of my life. I was an only child, and my mother died when I was fourteen years old. I lived through 9/11 just over a mile from Ground Zero. I went from being a public high school teacher who could barely pay her bills to starting a business in 2003, in the midst of personal bankruptcy, and growing that business to seven figures within seven years. I had also shifted gears in 2010, once I learned I was highly sensitive, and have maintained solid, sustainable seven-figure success while also honoring my highly sensitive needs for a decade and counting.

Throughout the pandemic of 2020, I navigated living in the epicenter during the early weeks of COVID-19, while still leading a global community of highly sensitives to not only survive but continue to thrive through and beyond the times—to experience business and life miracles *in spite of* what was happening around us. And I did all this while being forced to live apart from my sweetheart husband for the first eight weeks of the pandemic, because he served a vulnerable population as part of his position with the New York City Department of Mental Health at that time.

Yes, using my highly sensitive abilities to support me in rising up in the face of challenges as well as to be of service to others has been my calling for a long time.

And, yes, I have a sense that, deep inside, you know in your own way as a person who is also highly sensitive that it's been your calling, too.

Whether it be as an entrepreneur, in an organization, with a specific group, or in your life overall, you know in your gut you're meant to rise above the noise and the confused chaos of this world (in whatever way it shows up for you) to take charge, follow your intuition, and provide guidance to others—with options for how everything is now meant to be done differently from the point of this pandemic forward.

Because, if we're being honest, the old way in which we were all operating wasn't working so well at all: business marketing was about scarcity, community organizing was often about enabling, and self-help healing was about coddling.

Then as 2020 rolled into 2021, it became clear that those of us who are highly sensitive no longer have the privilege of time on our side to wade around in this old way of scarcity, enabling, and coddling. A quickening has occurred, and we are being called to rise above seeing our highly sensitive nature as less than, to rise above waiting to be given permission from those who are not highly sensitive, and to rise above the personal wounds of our past.

We are being called to say once and for all:

Yes, my way is different. Yes, I might be quieter than some. And, yes, I feel things deeply. Yet it is because of these ways that I'm meant to lead through these turbulent times, and the world will be in a better place because of it. I'm no longer meant to or willing to take a back seat to those who are louder or bigger. I no longer believe—even unconsciously—that this means they are better. My time to lead from my highly sensitive strengths has come.

Your eyes are on this page because you know that for you, too, leading as a highly sensitive is a call you're meant to answer, however that is supposed to look for you.

You know you're different, and that this difference is no longer something you're meant to hide. It's time to stop feeling confused and believing you need to fit in to the way it has always been done.

You know you're intuitive, and that now this intuition is meant to be your primary guide. It's time to stop pretending your intuition is less valuable than logic.

You know you're a deep feeler, and that these feelings are meant to inform you. It's time to stop being overwhelmed by the emotions of others and instead use them as motivation to act.

You know you're empathic, and that communicating with empathy is a superpower the world needs right now. It's time to stop ignoring what you know must be said.

You know you're a deep believer in justice, and this is the stand that must be taken. It's time to stop taking the back seat.

And let me tell you this: you're not the only one.

Which is why in mid-2021 it became clear that the time for the highly sensitive leadership revolution had come, and it also became clear I was not meant to write this book alone.

Everything I've ever created as a teacher and trainer has been in service to the highly sensitive entrepreneurs and leaders I mentor in the Business Miracles Community. So, of course, it's their experiences that are the heart of this revolution, and it's their stories that are meant to be the heart of this book.

Our message? You're not alone.

Read on to discover how you're meant to join us …

XO, Heather

INTRODUCTION
AND TERMS

by Lorna Lange
Business Coach and Community Curator
A Course in Business Miracles

IN THIS EXTENDED TIME of heightened emotions, fear, and uncertainty, having a highly sensitive nervous system has the potential for clear leadership advantages. And disadvantages.

Advantage: You are able to pick up on nuances in conversation intuitively. You provide exactly what is needed to support the other person while easily maintaining your personal boundaries.

Disadvantage: You are able to pick up on nuances in conversation intuitively. You unconsciously take on the anxiety, anger, or sadness of the other as your own.

What is the difference between these two examples? The difference lies in whether you are aware that your nervous system is highly sensitive and whether you skillfully manage it as a personal strength. If not, the likelihood is that you, as a person born with a highly sensitive nervous system, become a victim to that quirk of fate rather than a powerful leader of your life, business, and purpose in the world.

Most likely you didn't have anyone in your early childhood who understood about your especially sensitive nervous system and taught you how to be in charge of it. In this book, Heather Dominick thankfully solves the problem of how to get from feeling like you are at the mercy of your high sensitivity to embracing that you are highly sensitive—in fact, not only embracing it, but also using it as a superpower. This is no mean feat!

I know this personally, because I am highly sensitive and I have applied everything that Heather shares here. Just like 20 percent of the population, I was born with a more sensitive nervous system than most. I didn't know it until about ten years ago. And even though I've done pretty well for myself in work and relationships—I've had my own successful business since 2009 and will be happily celebrating my thirty-second wedding anniversary in a couple of months—I can definitely look back and see how I was often victim to my sensitivity rather than using it as powerful tool. I faked headaches all through childhood and adolescence so I could escape to my nice, quiet room and read. I literally took a year to crunch numbers before deciding to go into business for myself, hoping to get 100 percent certainty about my decision. Oh, by the way, the numbers didn't change from the first month of crunching through to the excruciating twelfth month when I was still crunching instead of acting on them. And when I finally launched my business, it turned out that the numbers ended up being pretty darn accurate. The former is a classic example of unmanaged highly sensitive nervous system overwhelm, leading to the need to curl up in a ball and soothe. The latter showcases the gift many highly sensitives have of attention to detail and how it can work against you when it takes a nosedive into analysis paralysis. Maybe you can relate?

The good news is that within a year of becoming self-employed, I found Heather and her training programs. For the past ten years, I've had the good fortune to be part of a community she leads that focuses on learning about our highly sensitive systems and, more importantly, actively training first to be able to manage the sensory overload we sometimes (or often) feel, and then to build from there to harness the power of being highly sensitive and use it to create a more fulfilling life and successful business.

Heather's nearly two decades of self-employment as a business coach who is highly sensitive herself and fiercely committed to ongoing personal growth and happiness in all areas of her life uniquely equips her to share her self-developed methodology with other entrepreneurs who are highly sensitive. But the programs go way beyond just her expert teaching. It is her consistent, interactive, finger-on-the-pulse-of-the-times support, and kind but firm personal guidance, that help community members actually feel safe to take action and evolve into the leaders they are meant to be. Even if that leadership might look different than what society tells us it should be. And let's be honest, if highly sensitives are going to lead the revolution that is needed now in our world, it's going to look different!

I'm not the only one who is forever grateful for the support I receive that allows me to be successfully self-employed, comfortable in my own skin, and healthier than when I started. In this book, you'll read real life stories from other community members about the transformation they experienced as a result of working with this methodology and the support of the Highly Sensitive Leadership Training Program. Hopefully, you'll get inspired to achieve your own goals by following their examples and going beyond just reading to taking real steps to implement what you've learned.

I personally know about the dedication to providing support and walking the talk at Business Miracles, starting with Heather and her business team. I'm not only a member of the community, but since 2015

I've also been part of that team, first as a business coach and then also as a community curator. True to what she teaches, Heather puts my unique combination of personal and highly sensitive strengths to work to keep an eye on what the community needs. With a range of support systems in place, from daily to annually we are in continuous assessment and responsiveness. Part of our longer-term support includes extensive curriculum training tracks that home in on more complex core issue needs of members. Even though lack of business success may seem like a marketing issue, for instance, we've found that for some highly sensitives, marketing is secondary to a challenge with relationships, mindset, or self-care. When we can get to the real heart of the matter and clear the blocks there, the business actions—which we also provide training on—flow much more easily.

As you may expect with any field of expertise, a special language has developed around highly sensitive leadership that is used within the community. So in my community curator role, I am providing you with a glossary to support your journey through the book as you engage with Heather's and others' stories. Enjoy the read!

GLOSSARY

AUK process–acronym for the process of transformation described in three stages: awareness of the issue, understanding of the issue at an intellectual level, and then consistently making choices based on your understanding and taking action on those choices until the issue has been transformed and embodied, which we call knowing

community (as a core practice)–consciously turning to an aligned community of highly sensitives who are interested in functioning at a high level when needing support as opposed to the common, unconscious practice of highly sensitives to either self-isolate or commiserate with others about how hard things are when you are highly sensitive

core practice—regular use of specially developed tools and approaches that support a shifting in mindset and effectively managing a highly sensitive nervous system

entitled queen—a skewed leadership energy of "I deserve" or feeling resentment about serving or selling in some way; it masks an underlying fear; one of three archetypes related to our mindset and behaviors with money

highly sensitive—born with a sensitive nervous system that processes stimulation and information very deeply, creating heightened physical, mental, and emotional impacts; 20 percent of the population has this trait (Wondering if you or someone you know is a highly sensitive entrepreneur? Take this free quiz: www.hsequiz.com)

privilege of agency—a healthy approach to making choices and decisions using discernment and setting boundaries and based on highly sensitive strengths such as deep thinking, deep listening, intuition, and ability to be excellent with language

regal queen/king—the highest leadership energy; recognizing that to truly rule your own kingdom (business and life) and take good care of those you serve, you also must be taken care of; one of three archetypes related to our mindset and behaviors with money

royal advisor—an archetype for an important role many highly sensitives excel at based on an ability to be excellent with details as well as to see the big picture and long-term impacts; examples are teacher, counselor, coach

scullery maid—a skewed leadership energy of servitude often resulting in undervaluing services and overworking; it masks an underlying fear; one of three archetypes related to our mindset and behaviors with money

shadows—highly sensitive shadows are unconscious ways of deeply processing stimulation and information that make things feel difficult and promote anxiousness; examples are perfectionism, overwhelm, shame, people pleasing, being judgmental, and digestive issues

shame shields—unhelpful ways we tend to disconnect from feeling and working through shame by either moving toward and flattering, moving away and hiding, or moving against and counterattacking

strengths—highly sensitive strengths are positive ways of deeply processing stimulation and information that make things feel easier and promote self-esteem, service, and success; examples are intuition, creativity, deep thinking, deep spirituality, and being detail-oriented

warrior king—an archetype for the 80 percent of the population that is not highly sensitive and approaches the world from a "more, better, faster" perspective without being negatively impacted by overstimulation; the royal advisor is key to the warrior king's long-term survival

CHAPTER 1:

ACCEPTING THE CHALLENGE

LET'S START RIGHT OFF by addressing two typical highly sensitive secret *plaguing* (and what can also often feel shameful) *thoughts*:

1. "There's something wrong with me."
2. "I'm overwhelmed and confused."

The research on highly sensitives, made mainstream by Dr. Elaine Aron starting in the mid-1990s, determined that 20 percent of the global population is born highly sensitive.[1] The important part of that sentence is "born highly sensitive."

Being highly sensitive is not something our parents did to us. It's not something we picked up on the playground. It's not because of that weird purple drink we had at a party in college. It's literally how we were brought into the world.

The highly sensitive nervous system is wired differently than the system of someone who is not highly sensitive. Those of us who are highly sensitive tend to be physically and emotionally over-stimulated more easily than someone who is not. Think all six senses: sight, sound, smell, taste, touch, and extrasensory perception. For instance, something that would be slightly stimulating to someone who's not highly sensitive (think noisy restaurant, strong perfume, or a lot of information coming at you all at once) is often extremely stimulating and has a great nervous system impact for those of us who are, often leading to the plaguing thought of, "I'm overwhelmed and confused."

So, if 20 percent of us are highly sensitive, this means 80 percent of the global population is not. Therefore, by sheer law of probability, most of the world is designed for the other 80 percent. Since most of the world is not designed for the highly sensitive person, most of us unconsciously had the experience at some point of being ... different.

Since most of us grew up feeling like we were different, we also grew up feeling like there was something wrong with us. We grew up not only *feeling* like there was something wrong with us, we grew up *believing* there was something wrong with us, viewing our highly sensitive traits as difficulties and something to be managed, to be hidden, to be ignored, to be avoided, to be ashamed of, or to be embarrassed about, often leading to the plaguing thought of, "There's something wrong with me."

As a result, our highly sensitive abilities have in many ways worked against us. We've developed ways of being in the world to simply survive and cope.

We missed the opportunity in our earlier years to really hone those sensitivities as the strengths and gifts they are. And as a result, we developed what I have come to refer to in my work with highly sensitive entrepreneurs and leaders as *highly sensitive shadows* and *highly sensitive coping mechanisms*.

WHAT ARE THE TOP TWELVE HIGHLY SENSITIVE SHADOWS?

According to Dr. Aron, our shared life purpose as highly sensitives is liberation. What's key is that this liberation isn't from the rest of the world, and it isn't from the other 80 percent; it is liberation within ourselves. Our liberation is from the self-imposed prison we create as a result of our experience of what it means to be highly sensitive.

This understanding comes with good news and bad news. The good news is that your experience of being highly sensitive isn't something that anyone else is doing to you. The bad news is that this isn't something anyone else is doing to you, meaning, "Yikes! No one else to blame here."

So, what we want to look at first is the highly sensitive shadow behavior we've all acquired in some shape or form, then the shame that gets triggered when we're experiencing those shadows, and then the resistance to the shame that kicks in and how that shuts everything down and prevents us from accessing our strengths, which then restricts us from being able to create what we want and lead ourselves and others forward.

Let's look at both the top twelve highly sensitive strengths and top twelve highly sensitive shadows.

HSE Strengths and Shadows
Strengths
+ Intuitive
+ Empathic
+ Creative
+ Visionary
+ Deep listener
+ Deep feeler
+ Deep thinker
+ Deeply spiritual

- Excellent with language
- Deep belief in justice
- Detail-oriented
- Acute awareness of subtleties (from environment to others' needs)

Shadows
- Perfectionism
- Procrastination
- Overwhelm
- Over-responsibility
- Over-protection
- Analysis paralysis
- Shame
- People pleasing
- Self-criticism
- Judgmental of self
- Judgmental of others
- Digestive/overall health issues

Personally, I experienced a whopping dose of all the above for the first forty years of my life, but the shadow I want to share a doozy of a story about with you is number 4: *over-responsibility*.

Like most of the highly sensitive entrepreneurs and leaders I mentor, I didn't know I was highly sensitive when I was growing up and so, of course, neither did my parents. In addition to being highly sensitive, I was an only child whose mother had died when I was fourteen and whose father was withdrawn and withholding as an attempt to manage his anxiety about this loss and life in general. On top of that, he then chose to live with three different women, one after the other, throughout my teenage years.

Though I couldn't understand and definitely could not name what I was feeling at the time, I could feel not only my roller-coaster emotions through these years but also all the emotions of those around me on top of my own—my father's anxiety and depression, the anger of the women he chose to be with, the irritation of their children, and so much more. When I tried to express what I was experiencing to the adults in my world, I was told I was too sensitive, too angry, and too dramatic, and that my expectations of others were too high.

This was painful, to say the least, but because I could feel the emotions of those around me but no one else talked about how they were feeling, I truly believed that managing everyone else's feelings was my sole responsibility. I also believed all these negative feelings were my fault.

One moment always stands out to me, even after all these years of therapy, coaching, and healing: I was in the car with my father's girlfriend at the time, being moved from my childhood home to a new town, new school, new house, new family. Looking back, I understand I was expressing my fear and anxiety when I said to her that I would need help being driven back to see my friends since I wasn't old enough to drive. She snapped and told me no one would be driving me anywhere.

I spent weeks apologizing, trying to make it up to her, and years believing that if I could feel what someone was feeling I was responsible for those feelings.

Here's what I hope you take from my story, and what's also generally important to recognize about these shadows:

1. Highly sensitive people aren't the only ones to experience these shadows. (Of course not.)
2. It's not about the fact that we experience them because we are highly sensitive, but how we experience them because of being highly sensitive.

3. There's nothing wrong with you for experiencing these shadows (of course not), but as a highly sensitive leader it's important to learn how to manage them as part of what it means to work with your highly sensitive nervous system on a day-to-day basis so you can be a steward of yourself, a business, a profession, an organization, a vision, or whatever you choose in your lifetime.

The third point leads us to the question: Will you accept the challenge? Will you accept the challenge to use your uniquely designed nervous system—a nervous system that makes you part of only 20 percent of the global population—to lead this world forward in the way that you are specifically being called to, whether within yourself, your personal relationships, your profession, your business, your vision for the world, or some version of all the above?

Lidia's Story

ACCEPTING MY HIGHLY SENSITIVE NATURE has been so impactful for me that I think of my life in terms of "pre- and post-highly sensitive."

During summer 2019, I was at a bank contract job I was grossly overqualified and underpaid for, and working there represented, to me, my countless failures to be successful as a full-time entrepreneur. Even though the commute was short, I dragged myself out of my apartment every day. Crying in the bathroom was a weekly routine.

Before I accepted that I was highly sensitive, I was in a constant war with myself and my environment. I knew I was an engaging, hardworking person with innovative ideas, but I would get only so far in projects before I gave up even though I had a slew of accomplishments—I created a groundbreaking product and founded a community of sex-positive women. But I achieved mostly through waves of beating myself up and drinking too much coffee followed by too many late nights. The physical and emotional exhaustion led to hiding, followed by procrastination, and then shame.

Out of one of these bouts came the result of achieving the bucket list item of being featured in the *New York Times*. The article was published, and suddenly I was being contacted for everything I ever wanted: a flood of product orders, requests for speaking engagements, and other collaborative opportunities. It's all I had ever wanted, and I froze. My inboxes terrified me, so I ignored emails and didn't respond for weeks and even months for some. And then, of course, most of the opportunities didn't pan out, which created more shame…

My tumult didn't just impact my work. It gnawed at my soul. Living in a state of extremes was depressive. Getting out of bed was hard (even though I was more creative in the mornings). I hid from friends. I ignored calls from my family. I constantly gave the excuse that I was busy. I had even gone so far as to hire someone to call me in the mornings so I would be on time to work every day.

No matter what I tried, I would end up with the same questions: *Why can't I get it together?* and *How can I fix myself?* Because something had to be wrong—with me.

Accepting that I was highly sensitive wasn't automatic. When I first heard Heather teach and so much about what she shared resonated with me, I still had reservations about accepting that I was highly sensitive. As a Black Latina, I had few resources about highly sensitive people I could refer to. I mean, I even googled it! I pictured the reaction of my family rolling their eyes. "First, you don't eat white rice. Now you're 'highly sensitive'?"

Furthermore, I ignorantly thought being highly sensitive meant I was weak.

When Heather introduced the Highly Sensitive Entrepreneur Coping Cycle diagram at a training retreat, I felt like she was specifically describing me, and I saw how much of my life was defined by resistance. Looking at that diagram, I felt like I could finally breathe and put down my guard, knowing I wasn't broken beyond repair. My nervous system was just untrained, and there were steps I could take to have a different experience. I could be free from the internal war I was desperately losing and have real power over the experience of my life.

I took a deep breath for what felt like the first time in a long time, and I accepted the challenge.

THE HIGHLY SENSITIVE COPING MECHANISMS

Before I share with you the highly sensitive coping cycle teaching that made such a difference for Lidia, let's take a moment to flesh out the three predominant highly sensitive coping mechanisms.

Pushing Coping Mechanism

Pushers feel frantic from not having enough free space or time for themselves, let alone to achieve what they want. Pushers will have a long, long, long to-do list and be almost addicted to getting everything on that to-do list done. Pushers will not slow down, but instead will pile on projects to make sure there's no possibility of even slowing down. Pushers will experience physical injuries or sickness, and will keep working in spite of being injured or sick. Pushers operate under a lot of anxiety. Pushers will get done what the other 80 percent can get done, but it will come at a high physical cost.

Hiding Coping Mechanism

Hiders are all about avoidance. Hiders are also rule-followers and people-pleasers. Hiders will do for others before they do for themselves. Martyrdom is a hider's best friend because taking care of others is an excellent socially acceptable excuse for not getting done what they need to get done for themselves. Hiders work hard to control everything in order to create a false sense of safety. Hiders operate under a lot of fear. Hiders will have all the right outer pieces in place but fall short when it comes to creating actual results.

Combo-Platter Mechanism

The combo-platter mechanism involves moving back and forth between pushing and hiding. The combo-platter is a massive act of not just self-abandonment but self-torture. These highly sensitives will find it very difficult to make any movement forward because it's as if they're pressing the gas pedal and the brake of a car at the same time. The combo-platter is the highly sensitive definition of insanity.

Here's where I am going to fully out myself as a recovering pusher. This was absolutely the way I survived from ages fourteen to close to forty. It was the primary reason I was exhausted most of that time! What was confusing to me was that I would look around at friends, fellow students, and colleagues who seemed to be doing what I was doing and often more, and they weren't needing to sleep half of a Saturday to recover.

I look back at that time, and the memories alone make me tired. Let me share just a few ways I was pushing my way through life.

High school: Even though my mother had just died, and I'd been forced to move to a new town, new school, and new family, I was captain of the cheerleading squad, editor of the yearbook, vice president of the Key Club, and involved in a youth theatre program while working a part-time job and graduating with honors. I know, again, this could describe any typical type A achieving, ambitious American teenager. Except I'm not type A, nor typical, and though aspects of this behavior helped me to not spiral down into, say, drug addiction, for me, these choices were self-destructive. I was dying inside and doing everything outwardly to try to ... well ... cope.

College: The pattern continued—more jobs and leadership roles, including starting my own on-campus theatre company and hurling myself across an ocean to study abroad. One time after my father and his next wife came to see one of my self-created, -directed, and -produced theatre productions, he said to me, "Heather, you need to stop doing and start being." So I added a heap of shame to the coping pile-on, because I could not stop. At that time, I truly believed if I stopped, I would die.

Graduate school and teaching career: I sense you get the picture by now, so what we can add on top of everything I have already described is a three-hour roundtrip commute every day to my first full-time teaching job that included a subway, two commuter trains, and a twenty-minute walk. Also, we can add a stacked social life that used the ever-beating heart of New York City to feed my pushing coping mechanism: plays, museums, events, restaurants ... again, all completely wonderful *if* this had been feeding me, but in truth (as mentioned) most Saturdays included staying in bed until after 2 p.m., when I would feel just recovered enough to get up and do it all again.

Self-employment: Of course, I brought all this behavior with me into my first years of working for myself, except now the coping stakes were even higher because my livelihood literally depended on it. I remember one moment in particular when I felt like I had left my body, and hovering above, I could see myself racing around my apartment like a chicken with its head cut off, plowing through my to-do list. I had the wherewithal to have the witness-thought, *This is insane, and it's going to kill me.*

Now, here's something that shows the fascinating way we function as human beings: whenever I teach the highly sensitive coping mechanisms and cycle, the pushers always want to be the hiders, the hiders always want to be the pushers, and the combo-platters always sigh wearily and say, "Can I at least just be one or the other?"

Let's acknowledge that one coping mechanism is not better than another and one is not worse than another. None of them are of service. It doesn't matter if you're a hider, or a pusher, or a combo-platter. All that matters is being able to more clearly understand how you tend to react when triggered into your highly sensitive shadows, what behavior you default to, so that from a deeper understanding you have the power to change the behavior.

THE HIGHLY SENSITIVE COPING CYCLE

To fully understand your predominant coping mechanism, we want to look at the highly sensitive coping cycle, which always begins with a trigger.

The trigger creates anxiety. You will feel anxious. Most likely, you won't even necessarily be aware of this because the experience of anxiety has become so familiar to you as a highly sensitive person that it actually feels somewhat normal, perhaps even an odd kind of comfortable. At the very least, it is familiar. It's what you know.

However, when triggered strongly enough, the anxiety will escalate to fear.

Fear then triggers a feeling of a lack of safety, and all this probably happens in a nanosecond. You probably won't even have time to take a full breath because it will happen so quickly and so unconsciously.

Next, you will start to catch yourself in the coping cycle.

As a hider, you will start beating yourself up.

As a pusher, you will collapse.

As a combo-platter, you will start to spin off your axis, disconnect, disassociate, and disorganize. You'll feel like you're going crazy.

All three mechanisms will then shift into shame.

From the shame, you will go into soothing. Maybe you will eat a chocolate chip cookie, or two, or three, or four, or a bag, or you may go shopping, or take a bath, or take a walk, or read, or journal, or go to yoga class.

Now there's nothing wrong with any of those things. There's nothing wrong with going to yoga class, there's nothing wrong with taking a walk, there's nothing wrong with reading, there's nothing wrong with taking a bath, there's nothing wrong with going shopping, and there's nothing wrong with having something to eat. It's about the way those acts are being used.

When they're part of the coping cycle, they are not conscious or proactive; they are unconscious and reactive.

Once you are soothed, you will start to recover and start to rebound.

Then you start to feel better ... until, lo and behold, there's another trigger. Somebody in a meeting says you haven't fully contributed, your spouse wonders when you're ever going to make more money, or maybe someone simply looks at you in a way that you misinterpret or says something that you take personally.

And round and round you go again, tossed like dirty laundry through the forever churning highly sensitive coping cycle.

Or, you can accept the challenge and learn to make another choice. Using energy management tools is one of the most popular teachings I share to help you do just that.

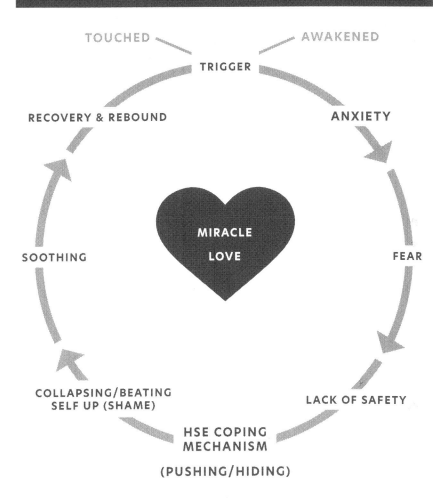

Melissa P's Story

RECENTLY, I went to visit my brother and his fiancé to see their wedding venue and meet her parents and sister for the first time. I was nervous because as a highly sensitive actor and intuitive reader living in New York City, I don't meet society's standards of success for someone my age. I was scared of being judged as a "weird loser."

I dread telling "normal people" that I'm an actor, because the first things they ask are, "What have you done?" or "What have I seen you in?" That question alone can often trigger all kinds of gut-wrenching insecurities, provoking a downward spiral into a pit of despair.

And then there's the intuitive reading business I started during the pandemic.

That topic tends to send people into their judgmental egos. I was scared they would think I was crazy—a crazy, weird loser. "Hi, I'm the older sister, single, unemployed actor/waitress/cat sitter/usher who sometimes just knows things and talks to dead people!" I thought maybe I just wouldn't talk about the intuitive stuff ...

One of the first things I talked about was the intuitive stuff.

I feel vulnerable bringing up this subject when I don't know where someone's beliefs happen to fall. I could feel a mother figure who had passed, wanting to be acknowledged. I was scared to talk about this knowledge, but to my delight, the family seemed to love the information! They didn't think I was crazy at all. They said their faith and spirituality is very important to them and encouraged me to share more about it.

Next came the dreaded actor question. For the first time in a long time, I wasn't triggered. I was able to take a deep breath and talk about the baby steps I'm taking in my acting career. I spoke about doing theatre in the past, about currently taking an on-camera class, and about recently upgrading my website. I even remembered that I booked a commercial during the pandemic!

When I thought about why I was able to talk about these things, I realized it was because I had managed my energy with an OFTU (Order Form to The Universe) and scripting before I left for the trip. The power of this energy management was why I was able to courageously share about my intuitive insights as well as stay positive as I answered questions about my acting career. I didn't spiral down into a negative thought pattern of despair like I used to.

Also, in planning this trip I needed to figure out whether to return home on Saturday or Sunday. To help me with this decision, I tuned into my heart and auto-wrote about my trip timeline. My auto-writing suggested I come back Saturday night to be ready for my podcast interview on Sunday. My intuition/guides often speak to me in song, and I kept hearing the song "Saturday Night Fever," so I knew Saturday was the day I needed to come back home. I decided to honor my intuition and return to New York City Saturday night, even though it meant I had to leave the weekend festivities early. I chose to take care of myself, and it meant I had to do things a little differently.

However, there are still some places where I miss the mark. I sometimes try to convince myself I'm actually not highly sensitive and then fall back into socialized patterns to try to fit in and not rock the boat. The few days I spent with my brother and his fiancé were so fun, yet challenging for my highly sensitive system. Not wanting to rock the boat, I did what they did and drank coffee and alcohol, which often triggers migraines.

Because I didn't honor my highly sensitive system, I ended up getting a migraine Sunday morning just before my podcast interview. In the past, I would have freaked out and gone into overwhelm and drama by canceling the interview at the last minute. Instead, I had already scripted and done an OFTU about the podcast, so I took some deep breaths and a pain reliever and got through it! I realized that in the future I need to honor my sensitive system more.

Overall, I left Saturday night feeling grateful to have met and spent time with these funny, sweet, generous people. On the bus ride back, for the first time in a while, I felt proud of the messy, unstable New York City artist life I chose, proud that I didn't choose a comfortable life. Spending time with people who have chosen a more traditional life path showed me that, yes, I am different but not less than.

I accept that I am highly sensitive, and I accept the very real challenge that I need to do things differently.

P.S. A few days after the trip, I received a new intuitive reading client from a referral. This client was experiencing an issue in which her family was encouraging her to stay in her hometown and get a stable job. (I know our families mean well; they are just scared for us.) I was able to share about my recent experience and the realization that I can accept myself for the highly sensitive being I am. I am still learning that sometimes that means we may have to rock the boat in order to honor our highly sensitive essential selves. During the reading, my client and I tuned in and connected on a deep level with joy and laughter as we chatted about what is truly in her heart. I felt so much gratitude to be able to connect with and help someone using my highly sensitive strengths because I've chosen to accept the challenge of being a highly sensitive leader.

ENERGY MANAGEMENT

The fact that Melissa chose to proactively manage her energy made all the difference in how she was able to lead within this family situation that otherwise might have been filled with a ton of tension for her and even have a negative impact on her work. *Energy management* is a term we use a lot throughout the highly sensitive leadership training programs, but what is it exactly? Energy management is, first and foremost, the willingness to take personal responsibility and be proactive about managing your highly sensitive nervous system rather than being reactive.

Untrained highly sensitives react to the world, allowing their nervous system to consistently be overstimulated. Most likely, they try to keep their nervous system from being overstimulated or overwhelmed by vacillating between over-protection and over-responsibility. When the nervous system is untrained, it is easy to be triggered into believing that because *you can feel* and experience a major intake of energy from others, *you are responsible for* the energy of others. This is how and why energy management is an act of leadership. You are taking personal responsibility as a trained highly sensitive versus taking things personally as an untrained highly sensitive.

Part of being a highly sensitive leader is understanding that circumstances are happening *for* you, not *to* you. Yes, this means anything and everything, such as things that are happening in your family, your community, your local government, or on a global scale, such as the pandemic of 2020. When you're managing your energy, you're able to access your strengths more quickly and easily as events unfold, versus getting overwhelmed and needing to retreat in order to process—and only then, possibly, maybe, being available to participate in any experience or circumstance.

Managing your energy becomes vital for highly sensitive leadership so you're able to be present and to be a contributor to your family, your business, your profession, your communities, and the world, rather than being a passive absorber. Energy management is important for highly sensitive leadership not only so you are available to show up and to be present, but to show up to present the *royal advisor* perspective.[2] If you're not present, if you're not available to contribute, then the unique royal advisor perspective you have to offer as a highly sensitive disappears. It goes unheard. It goes unexperienced. And then there is only one side presented, which is the *warrior king* perspective.

In my personal opinion, as a global society we are out of balance, and therefore energy management is important in order to be able to create a shift toward conscientiously created balance.

ENERGY MANAGEMENT TOOL: OFTU

Throughout the Business Miracles highly sensitive leadership training programs, I teach a variety of energy management tools to support managing overwhelm, shame, doubt, and other ways our nervous systems can become flooded, but there's one I've personally used for decades that always receives the most positive feedback. It's called the Order Form to The Universe. (You can adapt the language to use whatever word means "powerful life force" to you. I've seen "Order Form to God," "Order Form to Buddha," "Order Form to All Knowing," and many other iterations. Use your highly sensitive strength of creativity and go to town!) It's never about getting hung up on the linguistics, but instead finding the words that give you access to the purpose of the tool/teaching/training to support you in moving forward.

The development of this tool came from the early days of my business in the 2000s. I had absolutely no money but had learned of a coaching certification program that I knew was the exact right fit for me because it combined the spiritual with the practical.[3] Unfortunately, I had no idea how I would pay for it. I dug deep into my own spiritual practice and knew

18

that if I tightened my budget every single place I could I would be able to cover the cost of the first payment, though it would be very, very tight. From there, I made a commitment to myself that I would use everything that program had to teach me to be able to continue to make the payments month by month. So, though I didn't see the way to pay for the entire program before I enrolled, I made a commitment to create the monthly tuition payments month by month.

One of the most impactful trainings I received from that coaching certification program was how to more practically manage my fear on a day-to-day basis. It was the missing link I needed to help me take my own spiritual practice off the page and into the day-to-day practice of my business.

I took aspects of my personal experience with this training and adapted it into my version of the Order Form to The Universe, a tool I could quickly turn to in any situation to help me cut through all the confusion that was taking over my brain. Even though I didn't know at that time that I was highly sensitive, I knew I needed to keep myself from drowning in over-whelm with constant internal questioning like:

What do I do first?

What do I say to that prospect?

How do I make this whole business thing work?

And more just like that ... and I've been using it ever since.

Again, I've also shared it with literally thousands of highly sensitive entrepreneurs and leaders who all give me the same feedback:

"Thank you. This has saved me from myself."

It's a simple energy management practice with a profound effect.

The core of the practice is five main questions:

What DON'T I Want?
What DON'T I Want to Feel?
What DO I Want?
What DO I Want to Feel?
What DO I Want Others to Feel?

The sequence of these questions is extremely important. The first two questions help you clear your mind and energy. The third and fourth create focus, and the fifth question is the power question that brings it all together.

I highly recommended that you write out both the questions and your answers to the questions on paper (or at least type them), not just "think them." Really go stream-of-consciousness; let it all out. Be aware of how your ego-mind (the fear-based mind) wants to block you with "shoulds," "have tos," or "hows." Ask the ego-mind to kindly wait outside and stay with the practice.

You can put together an OFTU for anything that you're confused about, anything that has you in a state of confusion or overwhelm, any decision major or minor—nothing's too big or small for an OFTU.

What's most important is that using this tool allows you to show up as a highly sensitive leader rather than getting bogged down in confusion and caught in the highly sensitive shadows of overwhelm, or analysis paralysis, or perfectionism. Instead, you use the OFTU to tease out all the Do Wants/Don't Wants and Feels. This is you taking personal responsibility for and being in the process of training your highly sensitive nervous system.

ORDER FORM TO THE UNIVERSE

Order Form to The Universe Focus:	
What DON'T ...	**What DO ...**
I want ...	I want ...
I want to feel ...	I want to feel ...
How Do I Want Others to Feel?	
Next Inspired Action:	**Give Gratitude:**

CHAPTER 2:

TRAINING AS A HIGHLY SENSITIVE LEADER

THROUGHOUT MY LATE TWENTIES and early thirties, I worked as a high school drama teacher. My very first job was as a teaching artist working for various nonprofit arts and education programs in New York City. I was assigned all kinds of drama-in-education teaching gigs where one day I could be teaching in Staten Island and the next day I could be teaching in the Bronx or anywhere else throughout one of the largest cities in the world.

For me personally, this meant I was consistently exhausted and had no money. Yet, I couldn't understand why. The only conclusion I could come to was that there must be something wrong with me. I told myself I was so fortunate to have a job in the arts that came with flexibility and the opportunity to see all these different parts of my city that I would never usually see. I thought I should get it together and stop it already with the being tired, over-eating, and being the overall-mess-of-a-person I seemed to be.

I prayed a lot during that time for something … anything … to help me be like everyone else.

After a year of work as a teaching artist, I landed myself a job as a full-time drama teacher at a high school on Long Island, the second-highest-paying public high school in all of New York state, to be exact. (There were PhD teachers at this school earning six figures, and this was the late 1990s.) I was suddenly making more money than I'd ever made before. Yet, once again, I was consistently exhausted and had no money!

True, living in New York City and working on Long Island did come with a three-hour commute, as I mentioned earlier. That meant I had to be up and out of my apartment at 6:20 a.m. and on a subway at 6:30 a.m. to then navigate Penn Station, which had more people in it at that hour than a small Irish village, in order to be on a train by 6:40 a.m. I would change trains, which often included standing on a freezing cold platform, to get to the town where I taught. I'd have to walk twenty minutes before entering the school, finally getting to my classroom to start my day. The day would not end until anywhere between 6 to 9 p.m. (depending on the after-school play I was directing at any given time), at which point I had to do the commute all backwards before getting up the next morning to repeat the cycle.

So, maybe it did make a little bit of sense that I was tired, but believe it or not, I was not the only teacher working at this school doing this kind of commute. There were five of us. Three of them were at least ten years older than me, and they were all commuting enthusiastically for their love of city life and the Long Island teaching salary they received. Yet, here I was, still consistently exhausted and with no money. *What is my deal?* I would obsess. *Why can't I just get myself together??*

I spent my commute time listening to spiritual teachers like Marianne Williamson, Wayne Dyer, Caroline Myss, and Thich Nat Hahn on cassette tape, all of which helped shape my later ideas, though I didn't anticipate that at the time.

This agony led me to pursue another teaching job and to get hired at a high school that was now walking distance from my New York City apartment but came with a fifty percent pay cut. Yup, you guessed it: I was still consistently exhausted and now had fifty percent less of "no money."

By this point you would think I'd be able to see the pattern and my part in it, but it actually took me running away from my outer environment one more time to start my own business as a nutrition and wellness coach. (Yes, the irony is not lost on me that I was not living my healthiest life at the time.) The wellness coaching evolved into spiritual business coaching, where I finally got my relationship with money straight, only to then have close to a nervous breakdown along with my body physically breaking down. Finally, finally, *finally* I understood that I am a highly sensitive person.

This was when things truly began to change, because at last I understood how my nervous system operated differently than most people, which meant I could finally begin working with it differently. As I understood this and began to change not only where I was working or what I was doing for work, but the *way* I was working, my world actually began to change.

I was finally able to connect with the man I was meant to marry and to show up to contribute honestly to the work required of a marriage.

I was finally able to care for my physical well-being, stop the incessant cycle of gaining and losing anywhere from fifteen to twenty-five pounds every year, and feel energized throughout my days.

I was finally able to use my skills and strengths as a high-level teacher and facilitator in a way that gave me energy rather than draining me dry.

I was finally able to make much more money than I had ever made before and to—key point here—keep it.

I was finally able to take my work to a level of service that allows me to use my highly sensitive strengths to positively influence well-being and betterment for many.

Why do I share all this?

One, to let you know if you've ever felt bewildered about the ways you seem to process and relate to the world differently than those around you and you aren't yet sure why, oh gosh, do I get it—one hundred percent.

Two, to let you know if I can shift myself from feeling like a day-to-day hot mess to feeling the power of leading from my highly sensitive strengths in my business and my life, you can too. It's all about your willingness to shift from resistance to resilience as you train your nervous system to respond differently.

RESISTANCE TO RESILIENCE

The Business Miracles Path From Resistance to Resilience shows us the role that the coping mechanisms and coping cycle play in our resistance, as well as the highly sensitive shadow of *over-protection*.

Consider this beautiful story about a Buddha in Burma:[4] There was a massively large Buddha, twelve stories high, and it wasn't a very pretty Buddha. It was a quite ugly Buddha in the center of town. Because of a specific festival, the townspeople decided they were going to try to move the Buddha from its location in the center of Burma.

In the moving of this massively large Buddha, the Buddha cracked. Through the crack, the townspeople saw that underneath this ugly Buddha of Burma there was another Buddha made of gold. As they chiseled away all the clay and other not-so-beautiful textures that had been covering up this golden Buddha, what was revealed was that monks had covered the Buddha to protect it from any type of invasion or from any outside sources.

That story has always stayed with me, especially in connection to the "Big O" of over-protection because, as highly sensitives, we think we are keeping ourselves safe within the shadow of over-protection, when all we're doing is preventing our gold—our light—from being revealed and shown to the world. That is what the coping mechanisms, the coping cycle, and resistance are all about.

Stephanie's Story

I've always known I was a creative—a lover of music, theatre, dance, and the arts. What I didn't know is why I felt so different—like an outsider, always misunderstood. Sometimes I laughed a little too loudly, or cried a little too easily, or felt things so deeply that I learned to keep them to myself rather than risk judgment from those around me.

The confusion and hurt from feeling so different left me relying more on my own perseverance and determination to succeed than on community, friends, or family. I pushed myself to make things work and follow my dreams.

I also felt very alone.

I even went through a series of failed relationships that left me feeling like I cared much more deeply than my partner. I figured eventually they left because they must have discovered my secret—that I was too different. I wasn't good enough.

And yet, my determination to prove everyone wrong served me for years as I left a failed marriage, moved to New York City to perform in shows, found my current husband and moved to Maryland, and started my own business as a voice teacher.

What wasn't working was how exhausted I felt. All. The. Time. Even though I loved to sing and help others find the joy in singing, I felt like there had to be more to life than teaching forty students a week, working every Saturday, and trying to find even just a little bit of time to spend with my family.

Then, through a series of events facilitated by friends, I was introduced to Heather Dominick and the idea of what it meant to be a highly sensitive entrepreneur (HSE). The knowledge was profound and life-changing. I was amazed to discover there are other people just like me, who also want to be successfully self-employed, and most importantly, that I no longer had to do this all by myself.

I remember attending an in-person retreat with Heather and breaking down during a marketing discussion because, while so many other HSEs in the room were working through how to enroll more clients, I realized I didn't want even *one* more client! That would just mean more work. I was an untrained highly sensitive living in my shadows of overworking and being over-responsible. My highly sensitive coping mechanism of pushing to get things done often caused me to get sick—losing my voice or hurting my back—which forced me to take breaks against my will.

The most impactful learning for me at the beginning of my highly sensitive leadership journey was that I actually had a choice! I could do things differently than I had been doing them.

My determination kicked back into gear, but this time I used it to engage in the tools and trainings that Heather teaches and begin to leverage my highly sensitive nature in an entirely new way.

One teaching in particular that helped me streamline my business model was Heather's training on Time OFF/ON/IN. Suddenly I was working fewer hours while making more income and even more of a positive impact with my students and clients. I learned how to set boundaries within my schedule, freeing up my evenings and weekends (even though other voice teachers insisted they had to work those times to earn the income they desired). I then expanded my business to work with business owners and tapped into my highly sensitive leader strengths of creativity, visioning, and empathy, which supported me to hit six figures multiple years in a row while taking more vacation and spending more time with my young son.

As I became more and more trained as a highly sensitive leader, I had more ideas on what I could create for the next level of my ever-evolving business. I decided to write my own one-woman musical keynote, *Stage Dreams*, with nine original songs, even though I had never written music before. My story was woven into my show, and I was able to heal some childhood wounds in the process. I rented a theater and performed to a sold-out audience. I later sang songs from my show at conferences around the country.

I now had the confidence to do new and seemingly difficult things.

The journey of becoming a trained highly sensitive leader continues to this day. I am now clear that the journey is the goal. I continue to create new and fresh ways to monetize my skills as a voice and communication coach. I train and support people all over the world with an almost exclusively online business that I could never have imagined if I had tried to do this all on my own.

I am committed to my ongoing training as a highly sensitive leader because it means everything to have a community of fellow highly sensitives who get me, are on a similar journey, and are standing by with the support I need to continue to use my voice to make a difference.

Kara-Lee's Story

My Highly Sensitive Leadership journey started with a horse. Actually, it started with my heart, and following my heart led me to a horse. For over a decade, this horse had led me on a journey of leadership and personal development. Through multiple courses and trainings, I had studied with the "best of the best" and had become highly skilled in multiple leadership approaches.

Yet even after all that training, something still wasn't quite working. And like I had been doing for the previous forty-two years, I assumed it was my fault. I told myself, *I'm not in control enough, I'm not un-emotional enough, I'm not leader-ly enough, I'm not assertive enough, I'm not light enough, I'm not calm enough ... I'm just plain not enough.* Same old thoughts on repeat: *not enough, not enough, I'm a piece of shit ... what's wrong with me?*

By "coincidence," in summer 2019, I came across Heather's *The Business Miracles Podcast* for highly sensitive entrepreneurs and leaders. I started listening while I was driving to go camping and trail riding. The next day at my campsite, as I was grooming, tacking up, and getting ready to hit the trail, I started feeling the all-so-familiar sensation of rising irritation and frustration ... followed by shame and self-recrimination.

I suddenly thought of Heather's podcast teaching about coping mechanisms that I'd heard on the drive and realized *OMG! I think I might be pushing here!* So I paused, I slowed down, and I started paying more attention to what was going on inside me. I inquired of myself, *What might be creating these feelings of failure and not enoughness?* Just doing this gave me some breathing room and an opening to be more compassionate and curious by putting the shame and self-blame on a temporary pause.

At this point, I had invested more than six figures into my personal and leadership development, along with specific training in natural horsemanship, business, and finance, and I had sworn off any further mentoring. I had concluded that there was obviously something wrong with *me* that I needed this coaching support in the first place (unlike everyone around me), let alone that it wasn't really working to help me be the kind of calm, grounded, centered, certain, confident leader I wanted to be. I figured maybe I was just plain ole lazy or something. *For sure,* I figured, *something is wrong with* me. I mean, hadn't I essentially been taught that by my religious upbringing—that there's something essentially flawed and wrong with me? That we are all sinful by nature? That, without divine intervention, we are destined for hell? My deepest fear was that I would be eternally separated from God, and I never felt like I could be enough to stop that from happening.

Looking back, *this* is truly what a living hell is. These beliefs are what create hell on earth. That's what it's like, being a highly sensitive person, yet completely untrained. It's like living a hell on earth. Shame is such a disempowering, downright debilitating state. It makes me feel like I'm always doing something wrong and that I'm a bad person.

Despite swearing off more mentoring, something led me to become involved in Heather's program. Now I'm slowly starting to absorb the truth that the only hell I or anyone would ever face is an illusion of our own making. Shame and worthlessness are illusions; they aren't the truth.

Horses are like mirrors. Like all animals, they are truth-tellers. My horses show me the truth of what is going on inside. Now when I feel the deep shame, and when I'm brave enough to face it, I use the shame transformation tools Heather teaches, and I usually find a deeper truth. I feel comforted, I feel reassured, and I start to hear the whispers of love telling me I'm OK—that I don't need to be so afraid, that I don't need to feel so bad about myself, that it's safe to be seen and supported in a community with others, especially since they are also highly sensitive like me.

I've learned that this training as a highly sensitive leader is a journey without an end—a journey of learning to trust my heart, to trust my innocence, and that there is no externally guided path. Each of us is guided by life from the inside out.

Being trained as a highly sensitive leader means I trust the guidance of my heart even when … especially when … this looks different than what others around me are doing. Following my heart led me to the magic of my horses, and that magic has transformed every single aspect of my life.

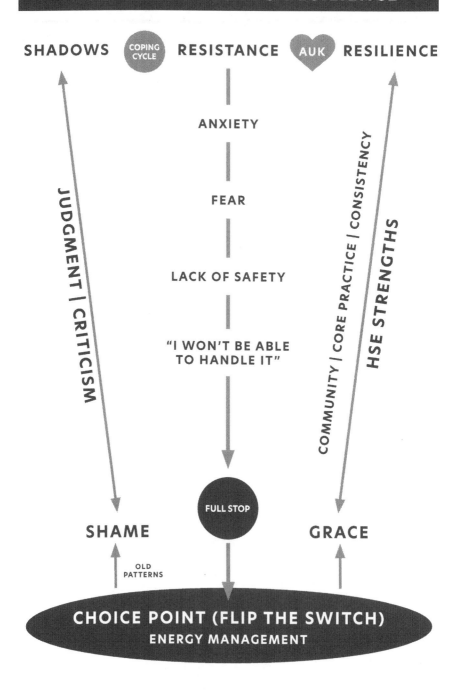

FROM RESISTANCE TO RESILIENCE

SHADOWS · COPING CYCLE · RESISTANCE · AUK · RESILIENCE

ANXIETY

FEAR

LACK OF SAFETY

"I WON'T BE ABLE TO HANDLE IT"

JUDGMENT | CRITICISM

COMMUNITY | CORE PRACTICE | CONSISTENCY

HSE STRENGTHS

FULL STOP

SHAME

OLD PATTERNS

GRACE

CHOICE POINT (FLIP THE SWITCH)
ENERGY MANAGEMENT

THE CHOICE POINT

Stephanie and Kara-Lee highlight so beautifully what I like to refer to as the "choice point" on the path of resistance to resilience. When we are untrained as highly sensitives, we tend to find ourselves looping around and around the left side of this path from shadows to coping to "I won't be able to handle it" to the shadow of over-protection to *shame shields* and, again, round and round we go.[5]

The key moment is when you hit that stop, even though intellectually you understand the actions you need to be taking to move yourself forward, such as writing a newsletter for your marketing, or inviting a prospect to an HSE selling conversation, or having a difficult conversation with a loved one, or turning down an invitation to a family gathering. Because you hit the stop and you don't write the newsletter, you don't invite a prospect to a selling conversation, you don't say no where you need to say no, or you don't say yes where you need to say yes, or any other form of taking aligned action, your shame shields become activated. These in turn can then potentially trigger you into a very dark, deep place, moving you into the highly sensitive shadows of *self-judgment* and *self-criticism*, and engaging with the Super Ego Voice (SEV), the voice in your head that is criticizing you, judging you, telling you all the reasons you have to be ashamed.

Again: resistance, anxiety, fear, lack of safety, I won't be able to handle it, stop. Stop is your choice point.

Every time you feel yourself stopped, it is not the be all and end all.

When you feel yourself stopped, there's nothing wrong with you.

Instead, every time you feel yourself stopped is an opportunity. It is a signal reminding you that you have a choice.

You can choose shadows, coping, and shame. Or, like Stephanie and Kara-Lee, you can choose the way of training yourself as a highly sensitive to access resilience through your highly sensitive strengths, such as the deliberate use of your intuition.

CHAPTER 3:

USING YOUR INTUITION — DELIBERATELY

ONE OF THE TOP HIGHLY SENSITIVE STRENGTHS that's available to you as a trained highly sensitive is the strength of intuition. But I like to take this strength one step forward in support of highly sensitive leadership with what I refer to as *deliberate intuition*, which is all about using your intuition with decisions, discernment, and determining.

First, here are several definitions for the noun intuition:

the power or faculty of attaining direct knowledge or cognition without evident rational thought and inference

immediate apprehension or cognition

knowledge or conviction gained by intuition

Second, synonyms for intuition include instinct, intuitiveness, sixth sense, divination, clairvoyance, second sight, and ESP (extrasensory perception).

Finally, my favorite, the antonym of intuition, one word only: intellect.

Here's what's interesting to me about these definitions and synonyms: there are many references to knowledge, cognition, thought, and conviction. There are also references to divination, the nonrational, or a second sight, but no connection or reference to feeling. I find this so interesting because throughout my decade-plus of mentoring highly sensitive entrepreneurs and leaders, I have received one question more times than I can count: "What is my intuition and what is my fear?" These entrepreneurs and leaders are asking about *feeling*.

FEAR VERSUS INTUITION

If we look at this question from a pure definition standpoint, we can see that fear is a feeling and intuition is a knowing. And even though the definition indicates that intuition is not intellect, it implies that intuition is a working of knowledge, a sensory knowing.

This distinction is important for you as a highly sensitive leader because it allows you to use your nervous system as an antenna. Yes, the wiring of your nervous system positions you to take in stimulation at a much higher degree than someone who is not highly sensitive. While your wiring can be used to take in stimulation and then interpret it negatively, which puts you in your shadows and fear, it can also take in stimulation and interpret it positively, which provides your strengths, particularly the strength of intuition.

Dan Siegel, clinical professor of psychiatry at the UCLA School of Medicine and an expert in interpersonal neurobiology, has famously created an easy-to-understand hand model that demonstrates the working of the nervous system and the connection to the brain.[6] The vagus nerve, which is the longest cranial nerve in the body and runs from the brain stem to part of the colon, touches all our major organs and connects to the brain, giving you access to the amygdala. The amygdala, in turn, provides access to creative solutions or, again, your strengths as a highly sensitive, including your intuition. In Dr. Siegel's model, first you fold your thumb into your palm, representing the limbic part of the brain and the brain stem (which includes the amygdala). Then you curl your other fingers, representing the cortex, over your thumb. This position represents when the brain is calm and functioning well. Now flip your fingers straight up. When you're operating from your shadow side, your "lid is flipped," as Dr. Siegel says. You're operating from the limbic response pattern, which is fight, flight, freeze, or fear.

This model demonstrates how the nervous system needs to be calm and proactively managed (back to energy management) for you to access deliberate use of your intuition, among other strengths.

Why can it be so challenging to distinguish between fear and intuition? It's because working with intuition is the opposite of the way the other 80 percent of people, who are not highly sensitive, operate, which typically gives credibility to intellect over intuition, especially in our pre-pandemic culture. Use of intuition is seen as a "woo-woo" practice, or at least a taboo, when discussing knowledge and decision-making as a leader.

Post-pandemic, everything is changing. We are in the middle of a disruption, yet disruption doesn't necessarily mean destruction. Instead, we are poised at an opportunity for transformation. Your intuition is available to guide you as we all chart our way through the long-term impact the global pandemic is having on our work and our lives. Your intuition is available to guide you to do it all differently than you've done it before, and to be able to do so without needing approval from others.

As highly sensitive leaders, we're here to be innovators, and it is your intuition that will lead the way for you into innovation. Those in denial are going to desperately be forcing things to go back to how they were. If you are looking for permission and approval to follow your intuition, then you want to ask yourself, *Who am I wanting approval from?* The answer is the people who are in that category of denial, the people who want everything to go back to how it was pre-pandemic.

Accessing your intuition and trusting how it is here to guide you will lead you to out-of-the-box ideas. It will lead you to creative solutions, and it will put you on a path that looks very different from the one you were on before the pandemic. Therefore, it will also look different than the path your ancestors have walked before you—those who have passed and those who are currently still living. It will look different than the paths of your colleagues who surround you. It will look different than the paths of your neighbors.

Knowing if you are on course will not come from looking around you at what everyone else is doing to see if you compare or "measure up." It will come from within you.

Now, let's take a moment to emphasize this is not an "either/or." I am not saying either you're intellectual or you're intuitive. This is simply bringing to light the ability for intuition to be accessed and credited as a source of knowledge just as much as intellect, and to be used as a deliberate leadership tool in business and life.

Chandy's Story

This is a story about my dog, but he's not just any dog, he's more like a miracle dog. For one thing, he is a hypoallergenic, nonshedding , small chocolate twoodle. A twoodle is a goldendoodle (golden retriever-poodle) plus schnoodle (schnauzer-poodle) mix. For another thing, he is from

Alabama, but now lives in Hawaii with me. You may or may not know that bringing dogs into Hawaii from the mainland is no simple feat. There are lots of requirements at any time, but the difficulty was compounded by the fact that I adopted him between September 2020 and March 2021 when some of the transit laws were changed midstream because of COVID. So this story about my dog is also a story about me as a highly sensitive following my intuition and experiencing miracles as a result.

The year 2020 was hard. By that summer, I felt tapped out and a little "blank" inside, just going through the motions of life and work, as I had continued to work all through the global pandemic because I am considered an essential worker. While my business was thriving and had undergone some huge changes from April to May, I felt like my personal life was missing something. I had my family, but no kids of my own. I wasn't wanting kids, but I was wanting *something*.

I distinctly remember one day, after visiting with a friend who had just gotten a puppy and then seeing another friend on Facebook post a picture of a new puppy, thinking, *Why can't I have a puppy?* I've always wanted my own dog but could never actually have one because of some reason or another: my mom has severe allergies, I was in school, I was renting a home, or I just couldn't afford one. But when the puppy thought popped into my head this time, it wouldn't go away. And it *felt* different than before. Plus, there was this additional openness to the possibility of, "Maybe I can have a puppy too. Why not?!?" So, I online-stalked what kind of puppy my Facebook friend had just adopted and who the breeder was, then Google-searched for other breeders in Hawaii. Here's the interesting thing. Before I went into Facebook stalker mode, I had no idea that this person had adopted a goldendoodle puppy. I had absolutely no idea what a goldendoodle was, or that it was a hypoallergenic breed. I just knew that I fell in love with the picture of that puppy, and so my quest began.

I started my search the same as any rational person would. I searched for breeders near me, on island and then in my home state. I studied their websites or Facebook pages for a few days at least, trying to suss out the breeders and their dogs, because if I was going to adopt a puppy I knew that I wanted one from an extremely reputable, knowledgeable, and responsible breeder.

Finally, even though I had some hesitancy and questions, I decided to put in applications to two local breeders because, again, "Why not?" As I waited for their responses (I applied on a weekend), I felt a restlessness inside, "something" urging me to do more research. So I did more Google searches for goldendoodles and somehow landed on the webpage of a breeder in Alabama. The site had loads of content, pictures, and videos and also connected to a Facebook page. It was a treasure trove of all things goldendoodle, schnoodle, and twoodle. By Monday morning, I felt great about this Alabama breeder and even more excited about the doodle breed as an appropriate dog for my needs. Now the question was, "What do I do?"

I really, really wanted a puppy from this Alabama breeder, but as I mentioned, bringing a puppy into Hawaii involves very specific requirements with a specific timeline that I couldn't meet on my own, and none of this undertaking was seemingly rational at all. I would need a whole lot of help. Now, because at this point in the process I was still in this amazing state of openness to possibilities, I decided to give the breeder a call and ask if they've ever shipped to Hawaii, because again, "Why not?" I left a message, and a week went by with no response. Undeterred, I tried again because, "Why not?" And what luck! I had this amazing conversation and learn that, yes indeed, it is possible!

What I didn't realize at the time was that the breeder had not only just been hit by a hurricane (September 2020), and was in the midst of hurricane cleanup, but was also caring for animals and, because of the lockdowns, managing many people who were wanting to adopt puppies. As a result, the breeder didn't technically have any available pups. That pushed out my expectations for the opportunity to adopt a pup, in my mind, by at least six to nine months. Yet, I was feeling intuitively guided and encouraged by this guidance I was experiencing. I put in an application anyway. And—surprise, surprise—one week later, I received notification of two possible puppy candidates, one of which was hypoallergenic and exactly what I was looking for in size, temperament, and color.

This is when the decision had to be made. In all honesty, a part of me kept waiting for the "no" signal to happen. The fact that the "no" never came was kind of a big scary deal, but I went ahead and said "YES!" anyway.

Fast forward to the end of December 2020. My anticipation had been building. The plan was for me to fly to Alabama to pick up my puppy on February 5, 2021. I'd been waiting for the last test results to come in to show that my puppy had passed and could be allowed into Hawaii. At this point I was fully expecting everything to go as planned. When I finally received the test results, it was with a heart-crushing blow of disappointment, as the pickup date was changed to February 26. Thankfully, with the training I had undergone as a highly sensitive leader, I knew I had help to get through it and I could handle it. So, I gathered myself up, surrendered to the circumstances, and adapted to the new pickup date of February 26 and the new entry date into Hawaii of March 2.

Let me explain the circumstances of this pickup with multiple flights so you can appreciate the full extent of this miracle. First, the week before I left for Alabama, there was a unusual and severe winter storm that hit the South, but it passed just before I left for my trip. Second, at the last minute, my sister decided she wanted to come with me, for which I was so, so, so very grateful because I had no idea how I was going to manage at the airports with my luggage, a puppy, and a dog crate. Third, the airline I flew on from the East to the West coast kept the middle row blocked on that flight, and so, because my dear sister was flying with me, we could secure all three seats in the row, allowing the puppy to be in the middle seat, partially sticking out. Fourth, because of the COVID-related changes to the transit laws, my puppy was too big to fit under the seat for my flight to Hawaii and had to fly in cargo. There was literally only one airline at the time that flew puppies in cargo to Hawaii, except they did not accept dogs in cargo that particular February of 2021. However, with my new entry date of March 2, I was totally OK—by two days! Fifth, to top it off, all my flights were on time!

When I reflect on all that transpired from Operation Puppy, I am in awe at the blessings and miracles that happened for me. In a unique and unexpected way, it demonstrated for me how the development of my highly sensitive leadership strengths, gifts, and talents have set me up to create amazing things. Before my training, this never would have been my perspective at all.

Oh, and in case you're wondering, I now truly understand why people love their dogs, especially twoodles, because my twoodle, Leo, was so worth all the effort!

FEAR VERSUS INTUITION— BREAKING IT DOWN

There is so much that I personally love and appreciate about Chandy's Operation Puppy story, but the lines that I think really capture my appreciation are, "…the development of my highly sensitive leadership strengths, gifts, and talents have set me up to create amazing things. Before my training, this never would have been my perspective at all." These lines demonstrate why distinguishing between fear and intuition is of utmost importance. And even more important is knowing how to deliberately use the process of distinguishing between the two in support of you, your business, and your life.

How can you tell when you find yourself in your own Operation Puppy moment, and you're considering taking an action that seems risky or out of the ordinary? How do you determine if the nudge to take the action is from a place of fear or intuition?

Years ago, just for giggles, I googled "fear versus intuition." And wouldn't you know that pretty much every coach out there, and every coach's coach, has a video on YouTube about fear versus intuition. I did not watch every video. (OK, in all honestly, I didn't watch any of them.) But what that said to me is that this is an important topic, right? This is a conversation a lot of people are wanting to have.

Also, in my opinion, I see that the conversation about fear versus intuition is meant to take a very different turn with the introduction of COVID-19 into our lives. Those of us who are called to be highly sensitive leaders are being given the opportunity, through this virus, to step off the self-help YouTube bookshelf and into committed, real-time engagement and practice.

It is one thing to talk about fear versus intuition on YouTube in 2007, which I think was the earliest video I found, versus what it is to be in practice with discerning the difference between the two as we navigate a global crisis, a.k.a. opportunity.

Let's break it down to basics:

1. Fear is a feeling of restriction and contraction. Fear has you wanting to pull away and pull back, avoid, and overanalyze.
2. Intuition is a feeling of calm and expansion. Intuition pulls you into growth and has you wanting to move forward … even when that pull forward also has you feeling nervous/excited.

So, then the conversation becomes, "When I need to make a decision in the face of something that feels fearful, how can I discern if I am meant to pull back from that which is potentially fearful or if I am meant to expand my experience by being willing to step into the fear?"

To help answer this question, let's go back again to the baseline definition of what it means to be highly sensitive, which is that we experience stimulation at a much higher degree than someone who is not highly sensitive. So that means that we, most likely, are going to experience fear much more intensely. It also means we can experience intuition much more intensely. But this is where things can get complicated. Because when we're discerning the difference between fear and intuition, if we're experiencing all our emotions at a higher degree, then fear can very easily override intuition.

Why is that? This is because fear is socialized. We have been trained to react in fear. Let's go back to the basics of being human and being taught from an early age how to keep yourself physically safe. I'm sure you had the experience, when you were a young one, of reaching your hand out toward something that was hot—say maybe the stove or a campfire or a tea kettle or a hot cup of coffee—and an adult pulling your hand back or slapping your hand, maybe even used a sharp-toned voice, and saying, "No, don't do that. That's dangerous."

In the same way that pretty much no matter where you grew up in the world you've had that experience of reaching for something hot and being told no, most likely you also *didn't* have someone say, "OK, here we go, little three-year-old young one. Here's how to use your intuition." This is why, as a highly sensitive leader, choosing to proactively engage in the process of shifting from untrained to trained as a highly sensitive is so important.

Melissa A's Story

I have deliberately called on my intuition thousands of times since I began my personal coaching journey close to a decade ago. Before that, I had only a glimmer of awareness of my intuition. I did not understand that it was always available to me as a guiding force, let alone how to connect with it or use it intentionally to support me. In the beginning, it was difficult for me to hear. Learning to do so was a gradual process; there was not one pivotal moment or click, and I am still in process with it.

I joined Business Miracles for Highly Sensitive Entrepreneurs and Leaders at the recommendation of my personal coach just before the fall 2019 training retreat. I decided that since, as part of the retreat, I would be completely on my own for four days, I would practice following my intuition in real time based on what I had learned so far from my personal coach. I participated wholeheartedly in the event, speaking and listening when I felt called.

I remember how it felt like fire was flowing through me when I stood up and connected with Heather for the first time. I shared that I was feeling overwhelmed in that moment, and Heather said to me, "Energy is *good*. Any feeling will last ninety seconds to ninety minutes."

Wow! I started to realize this "sizzling" part of me wasn't bad; it was just a part of me. And, I didn't need to be afraid of being taken over by my feelings because the energy would ebb and flow with beginnings and endings.

Throughout the retreat, I also followed my intuition during my personal time (Mexican food, walks without headphones, mineral baths). When I arrived home, I realized I felt restored versus my typical feelings of exhaustion from travel or socializing—a direct result of following my intuition. My intuition, my heart, knew what I needed!

I was now primed to stay with the process. I continued to practice following my intuition, but at home I struggled with taking intuitive actions in my business and when in the presence of others. I felt lost with wanting to have it all figured out before even starting, confused about my next step and whether it was the right one, and overall, I was overwhelmed by oncoming inspired ideas. But I kept reminding myself, *Stay in the process*, and I felt good about the progress I was making with learning how to deliberately use my highly sensitive leader strength of intuition.

Then, the global pandemic of 2020 hit.

In the first couple of weeks while we were at home, I kept hearing: "It's going to be four years." This short statement quickly grounded me to let go of any expectations of going back to normal anytime soon. My intellect and science background chimed in to confirm it was certainly possible the pandemic might take four years, but it was this inner knowing that supported me to relax into pandemic life, see what gifts it had to offer me, and keep going with my mission. My intuition, my heart, knew.

In a twelve-month assessment guided by Heather through weekly training roundtables in November 2020, I received a message from my intuition: "focus on doubling my impact, and I would double my income." I began scripting this daily. Through private mentor support with Heather, I was able to discern for myself which inspired ideas to commit to and go forward with, and the next steps to take, along with some solid account-ability to stay on track. This led me to develop virtual monthly offers for six months, serving nearly fifty people, while also learning how to market and promote events with intention. This led to several opportunities to serve clients one-on-one, eventually doubling the number of clients I was serving. And, in the first six months of 2021, I received twice the income of all of 2020—double my impact, double my income. Notably, most of the details of how these opportunities arose were not what my mind would have ever predicted. *Ever!* My intuition, my heart, knew.

As part of writing this, I checked in with my first official Business Miracles intuitive plan, which is a process Heather teaches to create a four- to six-month business plan by allowing your heart and intuition to guide what actions are needed to move your business and life purpose forward. Using this process, I clearly received a whole set of actions for taking my business to its next level. Connecting with my intuition now is easier; it's joyful and even a fun and exciting experience. Most importantly, I let all the doubts, confusion, and questions come up, as they still tend to do, but I see them differently now. My intuition cuts through this noise, and my fears no longer have the same power to hold me back. I no longer need to know all the answers or the whole path, just the next step. That's it!

I trust that my heart knows. "Welcome to freedom, Love," my intuition says.

COMMUNITY, CORE PRACTICE, AND CONSISTENCY

Melissa's story is a beautiful demonstration of what can change for the better in your business, work, and life when you're willing to follow your intuition. Yet, let's be honest, this is easier said than done, especially for us highly sensitives, because often our intuition is going to guide us to go beyond social norms, to do things others around us aren't doing, and as a result to stand out as "different," which, as we've already covered numerous times in this book, we tend to try to avoid since we've spent most of our life believing "different" meant "wrong." How do we navigate this?

We call on the power of *community*, *core practice*, and *consistency* to discover and develop our highly sensitive essential self over our socialized self.

Community: Surrounding yourself with a safe, nonjudgmental community of others who, like you, are creating what they want by doing things differently versus being isolated, lonely, and feeling like something is wrong with you or like you don't belong.

Core Practice: Using tools that teach you to shift from shadow reaction to strength response within yourself, your marketing, or your role in an organization versus constantly being barraged with energy and stimulation coming at you and feeling like you're one step behind.

Consistency: Developing the skill to move through overwhelm over and over and over so you are staying on course versus suffering from pushing to get things done or hiding and not getting anything done.

We call on these powers so we can have immediate access to our highly sensitive strengths, such as intuition, to create and lead our lives, rather than only cope and get by—so we can experience miracles daily, such as Brian and Macy so powerfully share in the next chapter.

CHAPTER 4:

DOING IT DIFFERENTLY

LET'S TAKE A BREATH AND RECONNECT to what we mean when we are talking about highly sensitive leadership. First, (you guessed it) the definition: to lead means to "show someone the way; be in charge of." As a highly sensitive leader, this specifically starts with learning how to be in charge of yourself physically, spiritually, and financially first.

Second, learning how to be in charge of your purpose: purpose within a profitable business as an entrepreneur, purpose within an organizational position as an employee, purpose within all your relationships as a person.

To do this, we must begin to understand and know our true self or, as I like to say, our *highly sensitive essential self.*

SOCIAL SELF VERSUS ESSENTIAL SELF

I first learned of the concept of *social self* from author and life coach Martha Beck.[7] The idea wasn't new to me, but I appreciated the way she framed it: "The Social Self [...] is the part of you that developed in response to pressures from the people around you, including everyone from your family to your first love to the pope."

She states, "Your Essential Self formed before you were born, and it will remain until you've shuffled off your mortal coil. It's the personality you got from your genes: your characteristic desires, preferences, emotional reactions, and involuntary physiological responses, bound together by an overall sense of identity."

Again, this idea wasn't new to me, but suddenly I saw this concept through the lens of what it means to be a highly sensitive person and, even more so, what it means to be a highly sensitive entrepreneur and leader. I partnered Beck's definition with a definition I learned from meditation teacher Tara Brach of trauma as repeated socialization[8] (we undergo trauma when we experience a repeated denial of our essential self) and thought, *Wait a minute! For those of us who are highly sensitive, this is really important. We need to look deeply at how this experience of social self versus essential self and repeated socialization plays into our perceptions of ourselves in the world.*

As you may have realized by now, I'm a big fan of definitions, and I love the dictionary, so one of the definitions of "social" is "of or relating to human society, the interaction of the individual and the group, or the welfare of human beings as members of society."

"Essential" is "of the utmost importance: BASIC, INDISPENSABLE, NECESSARY."

To really understand the meaning of social self, let's look at some examples. There's a person's social self-association with country: "I'm German, I'm Irish, I'm French, I'm Italian, I'm American, I'm Canadian";

or a state, province, city, or town: "I'm a New Yorker, I'm from Georgia, I'm from Hawaii, I'm a Texan, I'm from Montana, I'm from Alaska." Or there's association with a group or organization, or especially a school that may be a big deal in certain circles: "I go to this school; this is my mascot. We're Rockets, we're Dragons, we're Bumblebees." There is also race socialization: "I'm Latino, I'm White, I'm Black, I'm Asian"; religious socialization: "I'm Catholic, I'm Jewish, I'm Christian, I'm Hindu"; and family socialization: "We're the Joneses, we're the Smiths, we're the Dominicks."

SOCIALIZED TRAUMA

The specific categories aren't the crux of the issue; it's about what these categories have come to mean and, most importantly, the way we identify with the socialization and the meanings that we take on that typically were not generated or even consciously chosen by ourselves. The meaning may or may not actually truly resonate with who we know ourselves to be, deep down inside, in our essential self. But what's most important about the social self and socialization, especially when it comes to those of us who are highly sensitive, is that according to Tara Brach's work, repeated socialization is a form of trauma.

When you've been taught to do something and you've done it over and repeatedly because that's what's expected and accepted, yet it really goes against your essential self, the repeated denial of your essential self is an experience of trauma.

Here's where it is important to highlight the definition of trauma:[9]

A **traumatic** event is any disturbing experience that results in significant fear, helplessness, dissociation, confusion, or other disruptive feelings intense enough to have a long-lasting negative effect on a person's attitudes, behavior, and other aspects of functioning. Traumatic events include those caused by human behavior (e.g., rape, war, industrial accidents) as well as by nature (e.g., earthquakes) and often challenge an individual's view of the world as a just, safe, and predictable place.

Then also the three types of trauma:[10]

Acute trauma: results from a single stressful or dangerous event.

Chronic trauma: results from repeated and prolonged exposure to highly stressful events. Examples include cases of child abuse, bullying, or domestic violence.

Complex trauma: results from exposure to multiple traumatic events.

These three types of trauma also fall within a spectrum, according to the Davidson Trauma Scale.[11] The most common association with the term is on the more extreme side of the trauma scale, such as a horrific accident, abuse, bullying, combat, sudden and unexpected death of a loved one, or medical and natural disasters.

We can look at these definitions and begin to see the subtle yet chronic traumatic impact that would occur due to repeated socialization, including when the repeated socialization has you overriding your essential self until you get to the point where your day-to-day experience becomes, "I'm not really even sure who I am."

It can be easy to say intellectually, "Yes, I want to be my essential self. Of course, that's who I want to be." But when you're faced with making the changes you will need to make to be your essential self in all situations and relationships, the ego mind totally rears its head and says, "Absolutely not. No way. That is going to be dangerous."

This is part of the reason why we continue to engage in socialized trauma even when we come to an age when we are adults and we can make our own decisions: out of ingrained and often unconscious fears and limiting beliefs. We play out our fears and beliefs in all areas of our work and lives and then we're frustrated because things aren't working for us the way we want them to. Socialized trauma takes possession of our essential self, holds it prisoner, and buries it deep, deep, deep down inside us.

When Tara Brach teaches the trauma of repeated socialization, she tells this story that, to me, says it all. It's a story about a little girl who goes out to dinner with her family. The family sits at the table in the restaurant, and the waitress comes up to the table to take the order. She says to the little girl, "Darling, what would you like for dinner?"

The little girl looks up at the waitress and says, "I would like a hot dog and french fries."

The little girl's father immediately speaks up. "No, no, no, no, no. She's not going to have a hot dog and french fries. She'll have meatloaf and mashed potatoes and vegetables just like the rest of us."

The waitress then turns, looks at the little girl and says, "What would you like on your hot dog?"

The father is stunned. The waitress leaves. And the little girl says to her family, "She thinks I'm real."

As you commit to shifting from being an untrained highly sensitive to a trained highly sensitive, you are shifting from your socialized self to your highly sensitive essential self. As part of this shift, there is both the realization that you will need to be willing to do things differently, and a titillating freedom that emerges as you do.

Brian's Story

"Specialness" was what allowed for my survival in my early years—the specialness I was told that I possessed, especially by my father.

My father was sick with encephalitis from the summer of me being six. He died in the October that I turned eight.

He suffered with epileptic seizures regularly during this time. I saw him fall often, his big frame crashing to the hard floor. He began to scare me a bit then with his unpredictability. Yet my memory of him is that he told me I was special because I had a "spark" in me. He liked to call me Sparky.

I lived with this gift and curse that he gave me each day of my life. I knew deep down that the veneer of "golden boy" status was glossing over a deeper, more unsettling truth: I was different and I felt alone.

I was always told I was too sensitive, too emotional, or that I wasn't "a team player." Fitting in and doing everything to try to be like the others was my life mission. It was a mission doomed to failure.

Now I do it differently.

I am a man, a father to two boys, and I am highly sensitive. I have now admitted this to everyone but, most importantly, I have admitted it to myself.

One of the ways I use my highly sensitive strengths best is to connect with my spiritual guides. Without this connection, I feel ungrounded. In truth, without them I feel unsafe.

My father spoke to me in my writings during the earliest days of using the tools I learned in the Highly Sensitive Leadership Training Program for Entrepreneurs. I was in a time of personal crisis and looking for help.

I clearly heard, "I am, always have been, and always will be here with you. I am here with you now."

I thought he was lost to us when we buried him in the dark October of my eighth year. I know now that it was a confusion of levels. He was there with me all the time.

Just as I intend to be there for my sons.

Recently I experienced a magical day with my son. It would not have happened without my self-awareness of being highly sensitive.

I was busy. I was on the edge of defaulting to my coping mechanism of "pushing." I was about to overschedule.

Then I remembered my guidance, used the tools in the program, and I chose to say no to various requests for appointments.

This opened up the opportunity for me to teach my five-year-old son in his classroom with his friends.

It was the proudest I have ever seen my son.

His face lit up with excitement when I told him that I was teaching him that day.

I felt true joy that day working with him in his junior infant class.

It could not have happened without me knowing who I was, without me honoring my need to do it my way and to do it differently than what most people do.

To express myself not just in my writings, but in my actions, my decisions, my choices, and my internal moments of respecting my own truth has been the gift I have given myself by honoring my highly sensitive nature.

Being highly sensitive can feel like a curse. I struggled for many years to "fit in" the boxes that are created by society and that I created myself.

My father saw a spark in me, yet it took forty years for me to realize that I could honor it in myself.

I value this flame now that comes with the daily risk of being burned-out in the world that man has made.

I am humbled in the personal reality of needing more than this world provides.

Connecting to the eternal allows me to be present in the quotidian.

Letting go of shame around this as a father, a son, and a man is the greatest gift I could give or receive in this world.

THE AUK PROCESS

As Brian's story so beautifully demonstrates, following the path of your highly sensitive essential self is an act of courage. No question about that. The continuous act of essential self-courage has played a massive part in my own highly sensitive journey. It required the willingness to truly look at the thoughts, beliefs, and ways of acting that were passed down to me and that I took on unknowingly, unthinkingly, unquestioningly. I began to examine the way I was operating in the world because I recognized, *Wow! I'm not having the experience that I say I want. I'm wanting a different experience. Then what is it about me that needs to change?*

From this process, I developed a teaching I've shared for years to support myself and other highly sensitives in engaging and activating an expanded mindset that I call the AUK process.

The AUK process: "A" stands for awareness, "U" for understanding, and "K" for knowing. To fully transform from your current way of being in any area of your work and life into a new way of being is about going through these three stages.

AUK TRANSFORMATION PROCESS

Awareness

Understanding

CHOICE

ACTION

CHOICE

ACTION

CHOICE

ACTION

Knowing

First, you must become aware of the pattern you desire to change; next, you develop an understanding about what's not working about your current pattern and some options for how to do things differently. Then, finally, the trickiest part is to integrate the new way of doing things so much so that it becomes your "new normal." You have such a deep knowing of this pattern change that you have embodied it and now this is just who you are.

The reason this last part is so tricky is because people typically tend to stop at the "U" phase of understanding, believing that intellectually grasping a concept should be enough. Yet what lies ahead on the path between "U" and "K" is the *real work*—the willingness to take personal responsibility and engage in the core practice of making new kinds of choices and taking new kinds of actions over and over and over again until you've retrained your neural pathways to respond differently. This brings you into a new experience, a new way of being, a.k.a. what you've been *saying* you want. The process takes dedication and rewards you with exceptional inner freedom and peace.

THE REAL WORK

I'd been self-employed for about eight years when I generated seven figures for the first time. Being that I had started my business after filing personal bankruptcy, this was a very big deal. And—wait for it—surprise, surprise (or not), though on paper my business had crossed the million-dollar mark, you guessed it: I was exhausted and had no money.

What the what? How did this happen?

There truly is no mystery. As humans, highly sensitive or not, we are creatures of habit. Past patterns and self-made stories become ingrained neural pathways, shaping our experiences to be "same 'ol same 'ol," time after time. We want to believe that changing our outer circumstances will change us internally. If we just get the right partner, house, car, number in our bank account, everything flawed about ourselves will be forever healed and we will never have another problem again.

Yet, the truth is in the opposite. When we are able to finally engage in what I refer to as "the real work" of being willing to inquire, with personal responsibility, into what drives our thoughts, choices, and actions, and then through that inquiry begin to make true changes in our thoughts, choices, and actions, *that's* when our experiences transform.

Let's take a moment to talk about this phrase, "the real work." I started using this almost from the get-go when my business shifted to coaching and mentoring highly sensitive entrepreneurs, because it felt important to differentiate the inner-outer, deep focus approach I took with my clients from the more surface "coach your way to six figures in thirty days" approach that was blasting across the internet at that time in 2010. Also, interestingly, is at the point I started using that phrase I had not yet studied with Byron Katie. Though I'd heard of her, I didn't really know much about her, so it's of course no coincidence that she refers to the transformation she stewards as "the work," because our approaches are very similar.

The crux of "the real work" is personal responsibility and the willingness to cultivate the core practice of turning within to find the answers, rather than relying on a cookie cutter-generated formula to supposedly bring you what you want. This doesn't mean that outer actions aren't important; they most definitely are part of the process, just not the whole story. As author Meggan Watterson describes in her book, *Mary Magdalene Revealed*, "spiritual work ... happens where no one else can see or validate for us that we're doing the work. It's feminine, it's internal. It's direct experience. It happens quietly, within, when instead of reacting from the ego, we take a moment and respond differently."[12]

When we aren't intentionally and consciously engaging in "the real work," it often takes a big kick in the pants to get enough of our attention to motivate that change. For me, one big kick was pushing my way to generating seven figures only to land in the same place I'd been in so many times before. It was a dark night of the soul.

At this point in my self-employed path, I'd already created and was using tools to support myself in managing my daily terror and anxiety, and I'd already begun to bring my spiritual practice into my business tasks, but this dark night was what led me to understand that I am a highly sensitive person. This missing piece changed everything. Suddenly, how I managed my energy and mindset took on a whole new level of meaning—"the real work" level of meaning.

Instead of trying to figure out why I felt and seemed so different than the majority of people around me, on top of managing the daily terror and anxiety of being self-employed, I started using my energy management tools to be proactive about my highly sensitive nervous system responses. The more I understood why my nervous system responds the way it does, the more I could be "ahead of the game," or as I like to say to those I mentor, "roll out the red carpet for my nervous system." This way, I was a lot less likely to fall into my typical shadow traps of overwhelm, over-responsibility, and perfectionism.

EXPANDED MINDSET

If you are committed to change, growth, and evolution, then you will dedicate yourself to developing an expanded mindset. This brings us back to the importance of community to help hold you accountable to establishing a daily core practice and being committed to consistency to support you in doing exactly that. In the same way that you want to be engaging in consistent energy management, where you literally set up your highly sensitive nervous system to be able to operate at its highest potential from your strengths every day, you want to daily, continuously, and consistently be challenging your mindset.

This intent can be incorporated into your energy management practice, but it's important to go beyond only energy management to all the ways you are intentionally challenging your mindset, such as what you are listening to, what you are reading, what you are writing, and what you are creating that's visual. All this supports you in challenging your mindset every single day. Ask yourself consistently, *What am I thinking? What am I believing? How am I behaving that either is or is not supporting what it is that I say I want?*

"Insanity is doing the same thing over and over and expecting a different result." —Alcoholics Anonymous

If you are looking to have a different experience, you start by changing your thoughts and beliefs to support you in acting differently to bring about the different experience. You cannot expect to think the way that you've always thought, believe what you've always believed, behave the way you've always behaved, and experience something different.

What is important to emphasize here is, just as with energy management and the power of consistency, the same goes for creating the ongoing expansion of mindset. The process is not a "one and done." Energy management is the energetic form of going to the physical gym. Expanded mindset is the mental form of going to the physical gym. You don't go to the gym and take one yoga class or lift one set of weights and then look in the mirror and say, "Wow! I don't think that worked. Nothing happened." You go back every day until it's thirty days and sixty days, and then you look in the mirror and you say, "Wow. I do have muscles in my arms. Who knew?" It's the same when it comes to managing energy and expanding your mindset—every day, not one and done, and also not just when in crisis. You don't go to the gym just because you ate a donut and then think, "All right. That's good. I did it. We're done," just as you don't turn to expanded mindset suddenly because you didn't get what you want.

You give mindset consistent core practice, attention, and study so that when those moments of intensity occur (because they will occur, especially for a highly sensitive entrepreneur and leader) you're mentally prepared to think beyond what everyone else around you thinks. Then you're prepared to believe beyond what everyone else around you believes. You are prepared to behave differently than everyone else around you behaves. And that's the way you can lead in your business and your life as a highly sensitive.

Expanded mindset as a highly sensitive leader is a life of purpose versus a life of over-protection. It fuels you up and gives you the courage to be willing to claim your place among the 20 percent who influence betterment for others, whether that be family, friends, coworkers, or clients. And this is also the way you lead as a highly sensitive, not just to get more for yourself, though you will, but to demonstrate what is possible for others. According to A Course in Business Miracles, that is our shared purpose. It is "being the change." Not asking for, pining for, or journaling about what you want but being it.

Macy's Story

I have been a brow and permanent makeup artist for almost three decades. For most of those years, I was not aware of my highly sensitive nature. I didn't even know of such a thing! But as my business was growing and my social network was growing, everything started to feel a lot more difficult to me. I was overwhelmed easily, and people's thoughts, emotions, and behaviors affected me. I would take on my clients' energy.

Although having a business and being busy doing what I love was everything I wanted, it didn't seem to make me happy. It felt like I was always chasing success or what I was doing wasn't good enough. At the same time, I felt overworked and tired and as though I was always putting everyone and everything else first so I never had enough time for myself, both in my business and my personal life.

Over the years, my tolerance for different types of personalities and behaviors lessened. I struggled with difficult conversations and with setting and implementing boundaries and policies. I felt the misalignment, and that made me unhappy and in constant search for what was lacking. I felt like a martyr and an entitled queen, as Heather teaches, and I knew something had to change. That's when I coincidentally started working with an energy coach.

Through a four-year process of self-study, I discovered my highly sensitive nature and began to familiarize myself with these traits. Everything started making sense. I began to think, *There is nothing wrong with me; in fact there is everything right with me!* It was just that I was given a gift without a user's manual.

A year later, I joined the Business Miracles Community and highly sensitive leadership training programs to "get the user's manual" for being a highly sensitive running her own business. I started to train my nervous system with the tools and techniques provided to keep calm and stay connected to my heart and intuition. Now I am consistently using those tools and my highly sensitive strengths to navigate the ups and downs of the pandemic, such as transitioning back and forth between my business being closed to reopening, and dealing with and being around clients and people on and off again, on and off again.

In the past, I would have been stressed, overwhelmed, and worried about the future. I would have been coping and soothing in unhealthy ways. I would have been affected and triggered by others' behaviors and emotions. I would have been in major over-responsibility and guilt energy, as well as combo-plattering (pushing and then hiding).

Instead, in the past eighteen months I have been using my strength of empathy to offer myself, my clients, and everyone else compassion, while also creating healthy boundaries and taking care of my needs before the needs of others. I have been using my intuition and heart's guidance to stay aligned with my purpose and taking next steps even in the face of the unknown. I use my strength of deep spirituality to stay connected to myself and the universe, to be guided in every moment.

With ongoing guidance from the Highly Sensitive Leadership Training Program for Entrepreneurs, I have been creating plans to enter and re-enter working life, supporting my nervous system through the near-constant changes. I've been using energy management tools such as auto-writing and the Order Form to The Universe daily to stay out of overwhelm and get clear on what I want to experience today as things continue to shift and change—and to receive inner guidance and inspired ideas instead of searching outside myself for answers.

I can have difficult conversations, set boundaries, and ask for what I want or need without going into people-pleasing and over-responsibility. I can recognize and acknowledge my feelings and emotions, but I'm not overtaken by them. My relationship with money has changed, and I no longer feel uncomfortable about having the money talk. At the same time, serving my clients is now from a place of service rather than just making money.

I have created time for myself in the mornings for my routines and to enjoy the things I love before going to work. Instead of feeling like I have no time for anything but work, I now have time to work out, study, take my dogs for a walk, read a book, work, and live my life like a *regal queen*.

When I first joined Business Miracles, although I went in with 100 percent trust, faith, and openness, I still was hesitant and resistant to the idea of all the inner work and couldn't understand how any of it had anything to do with my business. But every transformational training in the curriculum has shifted and transformed difficulties and challenges in both my personal and professional relationships, resulting in more ease and abundance both in inner and outer results. I am happy for no reason. Everything happens for me instead of to me. Success has a whole different meaning to me now.

CHAPTER 5:
BEING OF SERVICE

THERE ARE MANY HIGHLY SENSITIVE essential self "trends" I've seen throughout the practical research I've conducted as I've mentored hundreds of highly sensitive entrepreneurs and leaders globally, but the hands-down most consistent one I've seen is exactly what Macy shares—the call to be of service. This is by far the biggest motivator for a highly sensitive to "accept the challenge" and dare to lead.

Yet, to do this, we must also be willing to forgo one of our biggest shadow tendencies: comparison.

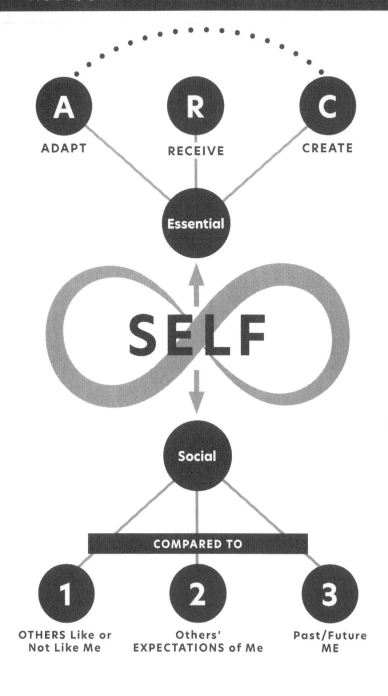

HSE COMPARISON ENERGY CHART

A ADAPT
R RECEIVE
C CREATE

Essential

SELF

Social

COMPARED TO

1 OTHERS Like or Not Like Me
2 Others' EXPECTATIONS of Me
3 Past/Future ME

COMPARISON ENERGY

There are three primary forms of comparison, as you can see by looking at 1, 2, and 3 at the bottom of the HSE Comparison Energy Chart:

1. comparing to others who are not like you or comparing to others who are like you
2. comparing to others' expectations of you; comparing yourself to the expectations that other people have, whether they are people in your family of origin, people in your town, or people in any clubs, groups, or associations that you belong to
3. comparing to your past self ("In 1989, I was able to do one hundred cartwheels in a row and now I can't. God, I'm such a loser.") or comparing to your future self ("Oh, this is where I should be, and I'm not there.")

All three forms of comparison, 1, 2, and 3, come through the socialized lens, the self who chooses to be socialized; however, when we have access to our highly sensitive essential self, this gives us access to an entirely new use of comparison energy, as can be seen in the upper half of the Comparison Energy Chart.

For example, when you find yourself in comparison, say comparing yourself to someone who is not like you, you have these options:

A. A: You can *adapt* what you're seeing for yourself and make it something that's really a match for your essential self.
R. R: You can *receive* support when you feel yourself in the throes of comparison energy.
C. C: You also can *choose* to take that comparison energy and channel it through the essential self into creating something that is for you.

Everything on the lower part of the chart is you trying to make yourself into someone you are not. The lower part of the chart shows, through comparison, repeatedly coming up with evidence to support the limiting belief that you are not enough: that you're not enough because you're not like others, you're not enough because you don't meet other's expectations of you, and you're not enough because you're not in line with your past or future self.

I don't know about you, but whenever I'm in the lower half of the Comparison Energy Chart, it feels like I'm in hell. And when I remember living day in and day out in the lower part of this chart, I remember feeling trapped and as if nothing was ever going to change. From this place of comparison, change can't occur for us highly sensitives. We will never be able to make ourselves into someone who is *not* highly sensitive. It's a lost battle before it even begins.

Nothing is ever going to come from this use of comparison energy, but you can transform this energy through the essential self, into adapting, receiving, and creating.

The infinity symbol on the Comparison Energy Chart shows that when you find yourself on the lower part of the chart, it doesn't mean, "Oh my God, I failed. It's all wrong," but that you actually have the ability to flow into your essential self at any moment, and that there will be an ongoing rhythm. You will be flowing in and out of your social self and essential self—again, not either/or, but a navigation of both/and.

However, the ideal is that you're living more in the upper half of the Comparison Energy Chart as your essential self, through the power of community, core practice, and consistency. A very simple tool that can help you when you find yourself in the throes of comparison energy via the social self is to make the symbol of the infinity sign by taking one of your fingers and tracing the symbol on the palm of your hand (another visual purpose of the infinity symbol on the chart).

You could literally be sitting and having a conversation with someone—maybe you're at a networking event, maybe you're at a family gathering, maybe you're just watching TV or on social media. You find yourself comparing yourself and not measuring up. Simply take an index finger and trace the infinity symbol into the palm of your other hand to support shifting yourself into the upper part of the Comparison Energy Chart, back into your essential self.

Geri's Story

I would have in *no way* thought that I was highly sensitive. I am approaching sixty-three years old and have been successful in service-related roles the bulk of my career, both in corporate and as an entrepreneur. I am not weak. I have confidence, I have a backbone, and I'm a team player. I don't cry when something goes wrong. I was always successful in any role, including in sales. However, being introduced to my soon-to-be mentor Heather Dominick, founder of A Course In Business Miracles and mentor for highly sensitive entrepreneurs (HSEs), came at a most fortunate time that helped me be in a position to grow my business by 400 percent in the midst of a global pandemic—from a place of confidence and the highest level of respect and service.

Here's how it happened. I moved from corporate, where I loved coaching and mentoring my 24/7 staff, into real estate in 2005 so I could continue to use my service skills and apply them as an entrepreneur. In 2009, the real estate market in Atlanta took a bit of a downturn. My husband, Kenny, is in the related construction field, which also took a hit, so when an opportunity came out of the blue to move back to a corporate service position, I accepted it. I was thankful for the opportunity, but I missed my real estate consultant/realtor work.

In 2011, Kenny and I decided to relocate back to Northern Virginia. My parents were aging, and they felt more comfortable staying in that area. We were glad to be back, and I continued in my corporate role remotely. Then in 2012, the company had a restructure, and my position was going to be folded into an existing colleague's position at corporate. I began to consider moving back into real estate.

I obtained my license in Virginia, interviewed brokers, and selected the highly respected broker I've now been with for more than sixteen years. As I established myself in Virginia, my sales were good, but I got to a point where I wasn't happy with myself or my sales, and I missed my mom, who passed in 2015, and so on. I needed a change. I needed to do things in a different way, and to make a difference. I wanted to set myself apart from the million other competing realtors out there.

That's when I met Heather. At first, as I mentioned above, I thought there was no way that I was highly sensitive. Then she explained the way highly sensitive entrepreneurs function differently, through twelve strengths and twelve shadows. When I read the shadows list, I was like, "Yep perfectionism, yep overwhelm, yep analysis-paralysis, yep people pleasing." Similarly, when reviewing the strengths, "Yep intuitive, yep creative, yep deep listener, yep deep thinker, yep detail oriented ..." So, I'm a highly sensitive entrepreneur all right!

Based on Heather's teachings, a *business miracle* is a change in perception. Now I know how to recognize when I am in overwhelm, or analysis-paralysis, or am being self-critical, and I can quickly change how I am perceiving things, so I apply my uniqueness and my highly sensitive strengths to provide a high level of care and service that exceeds my clients' expectations.

As a real estate consultant, I work with people who are looking to buy, sell, or rent their dream home in Virginia or around the world. They may be experiencing a major life transition but desire to partner with a real estate consultant they can trust and who will respect them, listen deeply to their needs, and powerfully guide them every step of the way. And as a result of our time together, they feel calm and confident that their real estate transaction was handled in both a personal and professional way.

For the most part, these relationships are very different from the usual real estate approach. For example, I received what I call a divine intervention referral. The client called me after finding my name "somewhere." There was a very, very delicate situation she and her family were experiencing, one that was very sad for all involved. I was able to use my strengths to make a difference, particularly with the highly sensitive strengths of deep listening, deep feeling, and my spirituality. At the same time, I was aware of shadows that my client was experiencing, such as judgmental of self, overwhelm, and shame.

Through that awareness, I was able to promote positivity, "flip the switch" relating to my client's feelings of embarrassment and shame, and have difficult conversations that were shared only with me. We were meant to meet and work together. Today she is thriving, and I know in my heart I made a difference in her life and her family then and now.

What I learned in Business Miracles about my essential self and my experience working with the Business Miracles Path From Resistance to Resilience allows me to promote success not only for myself, but also for my clients who are in their coping cycles. As I compare how I feel in my business now to how I felt in 2015, I know I am more confident, no longer comparing myself to others, my essential self is present, and I continue to experience business miracles. I love making a difference in my role.

There is so much more in Heather's teachings that I have learned about myself that I continue to apply personally and professionally. As I mentioned earlier, my business has grown by 400 percent in 2020 compared to 2019, even during a pandemic. I am so very grateful to Heather, her coaching team, and our community of highly sensitive leaders.

Ennis's Story

From the outside, it's easy to see my connection to "being of service." Most of my life has been dedicated to trying to make a difference.

Early on, I worked as a community organizer, then for a decade as a director in a nonprofit dedicated to fairness, health, and engaged democracy for all. For the past twenty-five years, I've led my own creative enterprise combining artistry and activism to engage people in critical social issues across the US. It's rewarding work focused on creating a happy, healthy, and peaceful world together.

Still, despite all I have experienced, what I've done never felt good enough to me. I struggled year after year to find a flow—to find my own happiness, health, and peace.

In 2019, I knew I couldn't keep going as I was. I didn't know how to change, but I knew I needed help. This is when I also learned about my highly sensitive traits, illuminating a lifelong challenge of never feeling fully at ease in the world.

Then I found A Course in Business Miracles. Really, it found me. I stumbled on Heather Dominick's work online. I took the quiz, got my report, and joined the e-list. Six months later, an email invitation caught my eye. It was time. I followed my heart, jumped in, and changed my life for the better.

In the Business Miracles Community, I learned vulnerability in showing my authentic self. I saw my over-responsibility and perfectionism and how it perpetuated struggle and scarcity for me. I uncovered fears and feelings of invisibility. I also learned how to transform my limiting beliefs and relearned to trust my intuition—the "whispers," as Heather says. I found my inspired purpose again.

I was ready for 2020—the most transformative year of my life.

Early in the pandemic, I felt called to hold space for anyone navigating the uncertainty of the time. It wasn't in my business plan, but that didn't matter; I was called.

Connecting the highly sensitive communication strengths I learned and practiced in the program with my mission gave room for an unplanned support community—a community deeply linked to me, to others, and to newfound clarity about what I *really* do in my work: remove barriers to activate inspired ideas.

The year of 2020 also called me to one of my most powerful artistic projects to date. At a Business Miracles training retreat the year before, I uncovered a surprising barrier I didn't know I had. Through transformation exercises that Heather led, I found I wasn't struggling with my business after all! I was struggling with a much deeper block to being an artist. This breakthrough realization helped me remember and begin to recommit to an artistic project started many years earlier: the "Freedom Phoenix."

Then in true 2020 fashion, the magnitude of racial injustice awareness and the looming election changed everything again. Primed with highly sensitive leadership foundations from the program and the breakthrough at the training retreat, the calling to channel a positive, hopeful message became louder and more urgent. I listened.

From March to October, I created hundreds of hand-printed posters manifesting an inclusive, restorative symbol of freedom inspired by our American eagle—a reminder of how beautifully complex real democracy can be. I wasn't sure how this project fit my business or my identity as an artist, but the calling was undeniable.

This work became a whole-body prayer. As I drew, carved, and printed, I prayed for freedom of expression and freedom to love. I imagined a beautiful freedom from fear for everyone. By the end, I printed ink on paper more than two thousand times.

I vulnerably (and uncomfortably) documented the process online. I offered posters to anyone who wanted them. This sharing represented freedom in its own right.

The results brought more than I'd ever imagined. Seeing the work-in-progress gave people hope during challenging times and inspired the creativity of others. I reconnected with old friends and colleagues. New understandings of my artistic work surfaced. People sent funds and gratitude, and shared the story—disseminating the message further than I envisioned.

Through these linked callings, I got the opportunity to *practice*. I practiced parceling big ideas into less overwhelming parts that I could act on. I practiced consistency. I practiced channeling something bigger than me. I practiced giving unconditionally. This, I learned, is the true spirit of being of service.

Being of service means listening to a higher calling and showing up. It means being where I'm needed most with a sense of purpose. It's giving 100 percent without thinking about it, without being overburdened by highly sensitive shadows like feeling not good enough.

When guided by purpose, my fears can transform into energy that supports something bigger, like freedom. This energy helps me easily support and be of service to others with flow. And that is real freedom … and that is true inner peace.

MAGNITUDE VERSUS LITTLENESS

Though being of service is one of our greatest motivators as highly sensitive entrepreneurs and highly sensitive leaders and is thoroughly rewarding as both Geri and Ennis so eloquently shared, it takes a fierce due diligence commitment. We must be consistently engaged in the process of shifting from untrained to trained and creating rather than only coping. This is why *Magnitude Versus Littleness*, a teaching that traces its origin to the spiritual and psychological curriculum of *A Course In Miracles*, is a foundation training in the Business Miracles Highly Sensitive Leadership Training Program for Entrepreneurs.[13]

Back in the early 2000s when I was first exposed to the coaching industry, there was a phrase I heard a lot: "Play a bigger game." I'm sure it's a phrase still used by a lot of coaches. Every time I heard this phrase, it didn't sit well with me. At the time, I thought this was because there was something wrong with me. I thought, *There's all of this talk of playing a bigger game, and all it does is make me want to run and hide. What's wrong with me?*

Now I understand that, as a highly sensitive person, I heard that phrase and my nervous system immediately interpreted it as pressure. As Dr. Aron states, highly sensitives don't just try to protect themselves from being overwhelmed, but they try to protect themselves from even the slightest possibility of becoming overwhelmed. Without understanding at the time what was happening with my nervous system, I figured there was something wrong with me if I wasn't out there playing a bigger game. Rather than this phrase motivating me (I'm going to give the benefit of the doubt that this is the intention), it plugged into my highly sensitive sense of feeling like I was not enough.

We always have a choice between the smaller, socialized version of ourselves and the more magnanimous, essential version of ourselves. Whatever choice we make will impact everything we do and all decisions we make.

When I first connected with this teaching from *A Course in Miracles*, my response was, "Wait, what? What? Hold the phone. You mean I'm responsible for this? It isn't happening *to* me?"

As with everything, mindset management is an ongoing process. However, being able to consistently return to the teaching that I already have what I want/need as core practice has provided a rock-solid foundation. I may slip off the rock, but I can always come back to the rock rather than feeling unmoored, untethered, and completely adrift, as I previously did.

This is where we remember how *A Course In Miracles* describes the Holy Spirit: that part within your mind that is automatically and naturally connected to your inner guidance, to your higher self, to the magic and the miracles of the universe at large ... That part knows what your function is. You already have everything you need.

Everything I desired, that you desire—the value, the worth, the money—was already in me, is already in you. Because it is me, it is you. My magnitude is what's natural to me. Your magnitude is what's natural to you.

What this means for us as highly sensitive leaders is to stop trying to be someone we are not and to instead tap deeply into our highly sensitive strengths and lead from this space. My magnitude, your magnitude, is within everything that is natural to us as highly sensitives. We are aware of subtleties in our surroundings, better at spotting errors, and good at avoiding making errors. We are highly conscientious. We can concentrate deeply. We are vigilant. We are accurate. We can detect minor differences. We can process materials to deep levels of what psychologists call *somatic memory*, which references how our bodies will remember even what our minds may forget.

We also are often thinking about our own thinking. We can learn without being aware we've learned. We are deeply impacted by another person's moods and feelings, and when our nervous system is trained, we can use this to make sharp, accurate decisions quickly.

We are specialists in fine motor movement. We are very good at holding still. We're more right-brained, less linear, and more creative in a synthesizing way. We are more sensitive to things in the air, able to imagine possibilities, able to be visionary, able to understand how complex life and death really are.

We are the royal advisors, counselors, teachers, coaches, historians, healers, upholders of justice, creatives. We are the balance to the other 80 percent.

CHAPTER 6:

ASSESSING AND MOVING ON

PROTECTING YOUR MAGNITUDE in this world does require vigilance. This is, first, about clarity, being clear that your highly sensitive abilities are of value. Next, it's about taking a stand for your highly sensitive abilities. Then, it's about trusting these abilities, and finally, leading with these abilities from a place of being willing to do things differently—differently than you've done them before, differently than others around you.

From the above paragraph, take a moment to highlight, underline, draw stars around or write down this most important word: *clarity*.

In this sense, clarity means what do *you* need?

What do you need to be able to operate optimally as a person who is highly sensitive?

What do you need to be able to show up in your work and your life from your highly sensitive strengths, such as intuition and empathy, even when (or especially when) challenged?

What do you need to be able to create your life rather than just cope your way through life?

Remember that, according to researcher Dr. Elaine Aron, 20 percent of the global population is born highly sensitive. Therefore, just by probability, what you need is going to be different than the needs of those around you who are not highly sensitive. How do you navigate that? How do you manage that? How do you unapologetically own that so you can be in a position to use your unique nature to lead?

As I briefly mentioned, my sweetheart husband, Stephen, and I were forced to live apart for the first eight weeks of the global pandemic. Part of his work at the time was with the New York City Department of Mental Health. He needed to be traveling through the city streets each week to serve a vulnerable population, and we lived in an open-concept, loft-like apartment. If he had gotten sick, we realized, there was no way we could have been together and isolated. This realization led us to scramble fast to quickly get him a second apartment. We were extremely fortunate and able to get a temporary apartment in the same building, and for eight weeks, we lived apart. The only time we saw each other was a couple of days each week when, while both wearing masks and gloves, we would take a walk down the street with only our fingertips touching.

At the beginning of 2020, never in my wildest dreams would I have thought I'd need to be separated from the most important person in my life in this way.

Finally, when we got the medical clearance to come back together at the end of the month of May, we knew we needed to make some more permanent changes to ensure safety through these times of uncertainty.

This led to us renting a house outside New York City, sight unseen, while also needing to rent a smaller city apartment so my husband could still be available for his work. All this led to lots of packing and unpacking and doing things that, as a person who had purposely designed my life to live as simply as possible in the midst of a city of complexity, I had said I would never do, like being responsible for everything required to manage an entire house, leasing a car, and shuttling between two residences.

Now, believe me, I get it. Out of all the stories about all the lives impacted by the global pandemic of 2020, mine is a story of privilege. Yet, here's what I really want to share: regardless of this privilege, through all this massive change, I experienced immense grief. Yes, we were privileged and, yes, we were making these moves for practical reasons of safety and, yes, I still deeply grieved the loss our lifestyle in New York City that was no longer there. I grieved for the loss of a lifestyle that I had worked hard over twenty-five years to build (going from being a public high school teacher and declaring personal bankruptcy after the events of 9/11 to being successfully self-employed and the consistent steward of a seven-figure business and mission) and that I dearly loved. Loved. Loved. Loved.

As we were moving, a mantra started going through my head that was relentless: *I didn't ask for this. I didn't ask for this. I didn't ask for this.*

Now, because I'd been developing my awareness of what it means to be highly sensitive for over a decade at that point, I knew to pay attention to this mantra. I knew to take this mantra into self-inquiry, using the tools I teach in my training programs for highly sensitive entrepreneurs and leaders—to dive a little more deeply into what this unasked-for mantra was all about. What I came to understand was the reminder of the power of what I refer to in my teachings as "both/and," meaning that there can be simultaneous experiences. I could both show up for this move with gratitude, recognizing 100 percent how privileged I am to be able to do this move, *and* simultaneously experience loss and grief and sadness for a lifestyle I loved.

As I stayed with the self-inquiry, what became clear for me was that my grief was about the lifestyle my husband and I had been living in a full-service Manhattan building for the five years before the pandemic. At that time, I had lived in New York City for over twenty-five years and had experienced lots of different lifestyles in New York, but the lifestyle I had worked hard to build and that my husband and I had been living for those past five years had not only satisfied me, but I had deeply loved almost every aspect of it. If you had asked me six months before the pandemic, I'd most likely have casually said something like, "Yeah, I really like living in New York City. #lovemycity." But as a result of the pandemic, I realized I *loved* my life, and not just that I loved it, but I became clear about *why* I loved it. It took a crisis to bring me to the clarity about why I loved my life.

And this is the point of my story. The key is the clarity.

Though I continued to experience loss and grief, that deepened clarity about what I valued about my pre-pandemic lifestyle became a beacon.

For instance, I realized how I so deeply value the neighborhood living that New York City offers. I valued being able to set up my life so everything I need is provided for me either within my building or walking distance but also the daily, multi-cultural relationship interactions within my walking-distance neighborhood. I realized how much I valued the straight-from-Italy maître d' who greets me by name and a kiss on each cheek before seating my husband and me at our favorite table in the quaint back patio, the straight-from-Korea manicurist, Jenny, who calls me sweetheart and leaves me with a hug after every appointment, the Turkish trainer who brought the newest form of strength training from Europe and set up shop just one block from my home, the Ethiopian wine clerk who shared the "yellow flower" New Year tradition with me. I could go on and on …

What shapes what I value might not match what shapes what you value, and that doesn't matter. Truly. Instead, what's important is recognizing that the inner influences the outer. It's about the essence.

Because I can now own that, this clarity will continue to allow me to find new and innovative ways to experience what I value in the here and now, though the specifics of that apartment building, that maître d', that manicurist, that trainer, that wine clerk might change.

But here's the real power of why this process of clarity was so important for me: what I realized I valued and loved about my New York City lifestyle is not what I was raised to value. As a highly sensitive only child whose mother died when I was fourteen, I unconsciously chose to subjugate my needs for the needs of my father in an attempt to not lose the only remaining parent I had.

For years, I had used my highly sensitive nature from a shadow perspective to be able to intuitively sense the needs of those around me and "chameleon myself" to mirror them. Whatever I sensed was of value to someone else, I would immediately shift myself to match. (This wreaked havoc on my early adulthood dating life, by the way.)

My needs barely existed, if they existed at all.

Here's what I really want you to get about this for yourself: what's important is the clarity about "what is of value to me," and it doesn't matter if it's of value to anyone else.

Take a moment to take that in. This can be a radical concept for so many, and especially for those of us who are highly sensitive.

It doesn't matter if it's of value to anyone else.

It doesn't matter if it's of value to anyone else.

It doesn't matter if it's of value to anyone else.

As I came to this clarity, what I also realized is how often over these past twenty-plus years since being self-employed, and especially since mentoring highly sensitives, I had held some shame about my love for my lifestyle in New York City.

Pretty much every podcast interview that I'd given pre-pandemic I would be asked the question, "How can you live in New York City as a highly sensitive? Why do you live in New York City *at all*?" So many people would casually share those subtle microaggressions. "I could never live in that city. It's so big and busy and crazy there." Any injury caused by these comments was unintentional. The interviewers weren't being malicious. I became aware of how often people share their judgments as a defense to not have to do things differently for themselves or to keep at bay something that has them feeling uncomfortable.

In my shadow of being a highly sensitive, picking up on the subtleties of judgment, I would go along—again, chameleon myself. "Yeah, you're right," I would say. "I don't get enough time in nature. Yeah, you're right. It's so busy and so crowded." Yet, as I spontaneously wept while packing and unpacking throughout my forced COVID-19 moves, I got clear about what emotions were mine and what were not mine.

My value for my pre-pandemic New York City lifestyle is who I am. I love living in a small, cozy space in the midst of a big, busy, culturally diverse, bustling city.

I love and value daily multicultural community interactions and building these relationships. I value investing in local services and businesses and having things done for me—everything from having a building staff member on hand who will come change a lightbulb to the expertise of my neighborhood tailor, and many services in between. This supports me in being able to manage my highly sensitive nervous system so I can then be in my highly sensitive strengths more easily, to channel my energy into being of service through my business and my life.

I also love living among history and curated parks while having memberships to museums, performance venues, and five-star hotel spas.

I love all of this! There it is. I said it.

From this crystal clarity, I will now do anything and everything to own these values, no matter where I am, and to create, step-by-step, my way back to this lifestyle in whatever way that's meant to look in this new version, new times, new world.

Again, it's actually not the specifics that matter. What's important is I now clearly know what's of value to me and I can be open to all the ways this might possibly be experienced going forward.

This brings us back to you: what is that deep clarity for you? From that deep clarity, you are then positioned to operate in your work and your life from a place of clear communication, negotiation, and creation.

Yes, this will require you to break patterns, give up on comparison, release highly sensitive defenses, make changes, and do things differently than you've done them up until now. Yet, as you are willing to step into what clarity is for you, to own it unapologetically, door after door will open for you. You will have access to more capability, creativity, and rich life experiences than you've ever had before. You will be part of the highly sensitive leadership revolution.

Gabrielle's Story

I came to the Highly Sensitive Leadership Training Program for Entrepreneurs after a long journey of numbness, disappointments, unfulfilled ambitions, and constant self-criticism—and after a burnout that stripped me of the very thing holding my pieces together: my professional identity. Though I had been stuck in my career for some time, I didn't have the inner resources to change. I believed no one could help me. I was too weird, too flawed ...

Change happened—*to* me. I became an entrepreneur—a rather strange idea! Entrepreneurs are usually optimistic visionaries who take a leap of faith to create a preferred future. But I believed I had no alternative. Of course, I quickly got stuck again. What was I supposed to do then?

That's when I encountered Business Miracles and the Highly Sensitive Leadership Training Program for Entrepreneurs. I had never heard of highly sensitives. I didn't think I was one. I didn't really care. I only wanted a *plan*, a step-by-step proven process to business success. I wanted to earn money—quickly—to calm down my terror of the future and stop beating myself up for being such a failure.

I enjoyed the beginnings of the training program: energy management, especially the tools of scripting and auto-writing, was very comforting ... and comfortable. I could journal for hours, reviving my old stories.

Then I reached the marketing trainings, where I had to act. I hit my familiar "wall of stuckness," and at the same time the 2020 global pandemic swirled over the whole planet.

At this time, Heather Dominick switched gears and brought adaptations to the program. Self-assessment took a large part in these changes because resilience and flexibility were required. The adaptations were about planning in a responsive manner, evaluating, and adjusting. I committed willingly.

And my journey into awareness started.

Equipped with the leadership training tools of the thirty-day plan, an aligned planning process, and the daily assessments, I started to document my activities and to look at things objectively: how I would get to the end of the week and beat myself up for not doing things I hadn't even planned to do, how ego-amnesia would have me believe I was doing nothing, and how my constant busyness was actually another form of numbness.

I leaned into self-inquiry, as Heather teaches, and the shame transformation tool. My underlying beliefs, the very posts supporting the prison of my ego mind became apparent: *I am not capable. I am not safe.*

As I grew more aware of these patterns, peace started to sink in. Energy management calmed my nervous system; self-assessment allowed me to understand I needed a way out. From this space of awareness, I could bring a new light to my destination and peel off the layers of my socialized self. Action became possible. I entered what Heather refers to as the "choice-action" cascade.

I began taking baby steps, assessing, and adjusting—small enough steps to avoid the fury of the super ego mind in case of a "miss take." (As Heather says, you get a take two! And a take three! And as many takes as you need.)

I'm still steadily building a deep knowing that I'm capable, that I can handle things. I catch myself falling back into the coping cycle: reacting to a trigger into hiding or pushing. I can't yet "flip the switch" in the instant. But through assessment and inquiry, I can now get out of a highly sensitive shadow quickly. It used to take days.

A story comes to mind. I recently caught up with a friend. She'd asked what I was up to, but I didn't feel I had anything to share on the business front. I could already feel the threat of her judgment. I shut down and nudged her to speak about herself, avoiding her questions. After the conversation, I slowly slid into the shadowland of super ego voice, self-judgmental hell: *What is wrong with me? Why am I so behind? How could I be so uninteresting as a person?* This time, though, I watched my mind also respond with curiosity. *That's interesting,* I thought. *How long will I be stuck in the coping cycle this time? Can I flip the switch?*

Later, when I could finally sit down, assess, and inquire, I discovered the switch had already flipped! I was ready to learn and decide how to do things differently next time. I had walked out of the pond of self-loathing with ease and poise and into the clarity of valuing my need to do things differently.

That's where I stand now. The journey is far from over. But it's OK because I'm safe, I'm in community, and I can assess and keep calm. And I'm even learning to love the process!

SELF-ASSESSMENT

Gabrielle speaks of "through assessment and inquiry." In the same way that the Order Form to The Universe is such a critical energy management tool because it goes right to the heart of what stops most highly sensitives from being high functioning, the energy management tool of self-assessment goes right to the heart of training your nervous system toward personal responsibility rather than taking things personally.

I first started using self-assessment in my early days of being self-employed, basically because I felt like such a failure pretty much all the time. Being a structured person is one of the ways I learned to unconsciously manage my anxiety from an early age. (Let me just say as a child I would often organize and reorganize knickknacks on my bedroom shelf ... for fun.)

I did well in jobs like working for a school system where there are clear rules to follow and a bell ringing every forty-two minutes telling me which classroom to go to next. Yet, I've also always had a strong visionary quality (which I now understand is one of our highly sensitive strengths) and would see how the systems I was working in could be improved, but hardly ever was anyone interested in hearing about what I saw.

Though it was this visionary strength that pulled me forward into being self-employed, suddenly everything was unstructured, nothing was predictable, and there was no one else around to tell me if I was doing a good job or even that they didn't want to hear my ideas. Even though I worked with business and life coaches or joined mastermind groups from the get-go of being self-employed, at the end of each actual day it was just me. And though those coaches and groups were helpful, the feedback I would often hear (wait for it) was, "You are being too sensitive. If you want to succeed as a business owner, you are going to need a thicker skin."

Though I didn't officially know I was highly sensitive at the time, instinctively I knew that "just toughen up" was not helpful coaching for me to receive. I needed something to support me with the process of developing these new muscles of being able to balance my tendency toward structure and my desire to create anew. Enter the self-assessment tool, which was an adaptation of a process I used with my high school drama students to teach them how to evaluate a scene through constructive feedback.

After a group of students performed a scene they were either rehearsing or creating from scratch, I taught their peers to give feedback by first sharing what they really liked and why they liked it, and then to share what they didn't like so much. But in order to share what they didn't like, they had to also have an idea for improvement to offer up at the same time. This allowed the students who had just performed to avail themselves of the feedback without getting defensive while teaching those giving the feedback to think critically regarding the feedback rather than only emotionally.

I took what I taught my students and applied it to myself as both "performer" and "observer." Use of the self-assessment tool is an opportunity to gather information about any situation or circumstance you've already experienced and look at it through a learning lens. Very similar to the OFTU, it is a simple energy management practice with a profound effect.

The core of the practice is three key questions:

What worked?

What didn't work so well?

Based on what I now know from the above two questions, what will I do differently next time?

I personally give credit to self-assessment as the primary tool that has allowed not only me but also the Business Miracles team and the entire community of highly sensitive leaders to grow throughout the past decades, and most specifically, to thrive through the global pandemic of 2020-21. Though it has also become somewhat of a running joke with the highly sensitive entrepreneurs and leaders I mentor that my answer to almost anything is "self-assessment," it truly is a golden learning tool because it supports you with two primary learning blocks that most highly sensitives bump up against:

1. Getting caught in self-deprecating stories, which then lead you down the path of either repeating unhelpful patterns or giving up altogether
2. Simply forgetting what happened the last time you were in a similar situation or attempting a similar task, which then also leads you down the path of repeating unhelpful patterns

This is why it is most important to either be able to take immediate action on what you identify to "do differently" within twenty-four to forty-eight hours of your assessment or to schedule for the future what you will be doing differently. This way there isn't room for forgetting. This is how you set up yourself and your nervous system to respond in a different way the next time around.

Khayra's Story

On November 8, 2019, I was on a London-bound flight from John F. Kennedy International Airport. As always, my calendar held the exact fifteen-minute breakdown of the whole forty-five-hour journey home to Saudi Arabia, including how I'd use my time on the plane to work and sleep. I was filled with relief to be untouchable in airplane mode, free from any request to help or reply. As I look back, I understand now that flights were the only "time off" I had to be with myself.

The bulk of my flight agenda was to engage in an energy management suggestion taken from the prior week at a Business Miracles training retreat, where I stood up in front of the whole in-person community of highly sensitive entrepreneurs to ask Heather Dominick for help on using the community's online forum to support my business. I had the habit of asking for help only in the last dire second.

It felt like my heart was shattered when her answer was that I would experience more success when I learned to ask for help regularly, not just when things were dire. It went against everything I ever learned about being independent. It went against everything I learned about having self-esteem. How could I prove myself while asking for help regularly about every little thing? What would I even ask about?

She suggested I complete one of the program's energy management tools, an Order Form to The Universe (OFTU), on what I wanted from life and to get clarity on what to ask on the forum. I put it on my calendar to do on the plane.

After having gone through every item of my usual takeoff routine, I sat with my pad of paper in front of me and began filling out the order form on what I wanted from every compartment of my life. It added up to thirteen OFTUs covering personal life, three roles in my full-time job, three volunteer roles, four roles making up my side hustle, and the Business Miracles program itself. It was only later I found that she expected me to complete just one OFTU.

Looking at these thirteen pages, massaging my wrists because of the tension in my writing, I noticed how ignorant I had been of what was happening in my life commitments. I could finally see that every day was a struggle to get out of bed because I wouldn't go to sleep until 2:00 a.m. so I could finish my to-do list. I would "calm down" when I filled myself up with caffeine and adrenaline to rush to work. The only socializing I did in my hip workplace was to remember people's names, which I did because I needed my volunteer roles to succeed. In the evening, I'd rush to a support group I was leading, furiously organizing the next one on my phone in the car. On Friday, my "day off," I'd sneak in work on my phone and engage with family as a coordinator and favor-giver. Saturday was my self-employment day when I would coach clients for cheap or barter.

As I landed in London, I made a commitment: It was time to take baby steps and let go of this unrealistic way of living.

I used multiple elements of the Business Miracles highly sensitive leadership training program, including the forum, to take those baby steps. I challenged myself to use the shame transformation tools weekly, getting clear that my overcommitments came from either shameful agreement or rebellion. I joined the team leader series training, where I learned stating my needs and my boundaries was the kindest act for my team members and contractors. I was witnessed and supported in my on-again, off-again journey to master time off.

In between these enlightened actions was a resistance I can't put into words. But through the support of the program, I always re-returned and took another baby step.

Since that flight, I've gotten to know myself through many

self-assessments and found my strengths lie in problem-solving, connecting, and leadership. So, what my untrained highly sensitive self was trying to make work in this hectic lifestyle was using those strengths fully through a large assortment of projects. What did not work was my lifelong underlying belief, unknown to me at the time, that the only permission I could have to flex my strengths was through compartmentalized commitments that caused me exhaustion and no actual time off.

Three years later, I now have only one full-time business where I put all my strengths to use. Clients pay in full and stick to our agreements. I take three full days off a week that act as my personal "airplane mode." I have only one volunteer commitment that helps me develop myself instead of proving myself. Every month, I go through the self-assessment process to find my next baby step in becoming a human being instead of a human doing.

And, every day, for this year's daily energy management, I get clear on what I want from life using just *one* OFTU for the day.

GOOD ENOUGH BUSINESS

Developing the ability to keep things focused by assessing and moving on, as Khayra highlights in her story, is a core practice of shifting from "not enough" to "good enough" for us highly sensitive entrepreneurs and leaders.

There is a child psychology theory from British pediatrician and psychoanalyst D.W. Winnicott, called the *good enough mother*. It's from his book, *Playing and Reality*. According to Winnicott, being a good enough mother means balancing between giving an infant what they need, and helping them to learn that not all needs are instantly met.[14] Good enough mothering is the child being able to be OK with not having everything provided all the time, all at once.

The good enough mother is supporting the child with learning to be OK with not having everything provided all the time so that eventually the child develops her own agency to choose. That's the important part. Eventually the child will learn to choose because she doesn't expect to have everything given to her, and done for her, all the time and immediately.

I had been aware of this theory for a long time, having studied psychology in undergraduate school. And then, in 2019, I read an article in the *New York Times* called "The Good Enough Life."[15] The article was basically another angle on a trend observation of how globally we have become a culture that feels something is wrong if we can't have our needs instantaneously met. The article about "The Good Enough Life" had me thinking about "the good enough business."

I asked myself what that might look like? How might that feel? How might that transform the highly sensitive tendency to gravitate toward "What's wrong with me?" "Why am I not good enough?" and "Why do I have shame for being who I am?" And how might the concept of the good enough business shortcut the need for shame shields? What could that look like?

The good enough business speaks to feeling shame because your business is not making enough money yet, shame because your growth pace is different, or shame because your business doesn't look like other businesses in your industry or what you see on social media. It speaks to all the ways I've watched for years highly sensitive entrepreneurs beat themselves up for all these reasons and more. Not enough. Not enough. Not enough. What if where you are right now is good enough? What if you accept where you are right now as good enough?

Now, very likely your ego mind is responding, "What? If I accept where I am right now as good enough, how will I ever get anything done? How will I ever get further than where I am right now?"

And my response is this: How is beating up on yourself working for you? How is that moving you along? How has that got you accelerating?

Are you happy? Are you feeling good? What if you took all that "beating up on self" energy and put it into the good enough business? And what if you got to use *privilege of agency* to decide what that is for you? Lisa gets to decide what it is for her. Jen gets to decide what it is for her. Manon gets to decide what it is for her. Celeste gets to decide what it is for her. And Celeste's doesn't look like Nova's. It's not supposed to. And Celeste's doesn't look like all those who are out there posting on social media where we really have no idea what's going on behind closed doors. What if you could use privilege of agency to design your business from your essential self and let it be good enough? Where's the shame in that?

PRIVILEGE OF AGENCY

A *privilege* is a special right, an advantage or immunity granted, available only to a particular person or group.

In social science, *agency* is defined as the capacity to act independently and to make our own free choices. One's agency is one's independent capability or ability to act on one's will.

Privilege of agency, therefore, is a healthy approach to making decisions, using discernment, and setting boundaries based on your highly sensitive strengths, such as the strengths of deep thinking, deep listening, intuition, and the ability to be excellent with language. Privilege of agency is the gateway to your highly sensitive essential self—taking the opportunity to look very deeply at every decision you make, even tiny decisions, and looking at whether a choice is made because that's what was expected to be done, because that's what always has been done, or instead because it was chosen based on your special right and ability to act independently.

Let me give you an everyday example: hair appointments. In 2016, when I was dealing with some intense health issues, I would schedule a hair appointment, and then I wouldn't feel well enough to go. And so, I would need to call and cancel at the last minute. With that type of service, like a lot of others, if you call and cancel last minute, you're still obligated to pay. In the past, I would have pushed myself to go. I would have gone into my highly sensitive coping mechanism of pushing, and the socialized behavior, to make sure that I made the appointment even if it wasn't in my best interest.

Also, in the past, if I couldn't push myself to get there (although as a recovering pusher, that's typically what I would do), I would shift into either an irate version of the money mindset archetype of the entitled queen. "I can't believe they have this type of policy. I'm getting charged. That's ridiculous." Or I would slip into the money mindset archetype of scullery maid and beat myself up. "What's wrong with you? Why can't you just get there? Anyone who is normal wouldn't have to cancel this appointment. Just get yourself on the subway. Stop being such a baby."

With the activation of privilege of agency, the decision is mine. The choice sounds like, "I'm not going to push myself. It's not in my best interest to make it to this appointment. I respect policies, because I respect myself, so I respect others and their policies. So I happily pay for that appointment that I'm not going to be able to get to."

That's privilege of agency.

From here, let's also look at what privilege of agency is not. Privilege of agency is not an excuse to act out from your shame shield of *against, toward, or away*. Privilege of agency is not permission to be aggressive by lashing out. Privilege of agency is not permission to be passive aggressive by avoiding. Privilege of agency is not permission to blame or shame others or yourself. Privilege of agency is not an excuse to go into hiding, pushing, or combo-plattering as a way of coping. Privilege of agency is not justification for shadow behavior of people pleasing, perfectionism, analysis-paralysis, over-responsibility, over-protection, or any other shadow behavior.

Why, then, is privilege of agency important for us as highly sensitive entrepreneurs and leaders? It's important for us because our nervous systems are wired differently. A lot of the time, what you need for your well-being and to operate at your ultimate best is different than what those around you need, which means your decisions are going to be different than those of others around you. And that's more than OK.

CHAPTER 7:

WASH, RINSE, REST, REPEAT

THE SHIFT FROM HIGHLY SENSITIVE shame or shadows to strengths, or from coping to creating, or from resistance to resilience, is not something you "arrive at" and never have to do again. Instead, shifting from a shadow behavior to a strength behavior is a muscle you want to build so you have access to it more easily, more quickly, and more often.

We're not looking to eradicate shadows, in the same way that we talked about how the coping cycle or your coping mechanisms are not bad. We want to strengthen the muscle, so you can more easily, more quickly, and more often catch yourself in shadow behavior and create the shift to strengths.

Why is this important? Shifting more quickly to strengths makes everything more productive, and creative, and fruitful—from business or work to every aspect of life, including all your most important relationships.

SHADOW TO STRENGTH PATHWAYS

To help you be able to develop that muscle, to develop that skill, to be able to shift from shadow to strength, I would like to introduce you to the HSE Shadow to Strength Pathways.

I'd like to focus first on the "drama" aspect of the Shadow to Strength Pathways. This comes from a theory and teaching referred to as the Karpman drama triangle, which is a social model of human interaction created by Steven B. Karpman.[16] The Karpman triangle is often also referred to as DDT, which stands for the dreaded drama triangle. This triangle maps a type of destructive interaction that occurs among people in conflict. It also refers to *intrapersonal* conflict, meaning conflict within yourself.

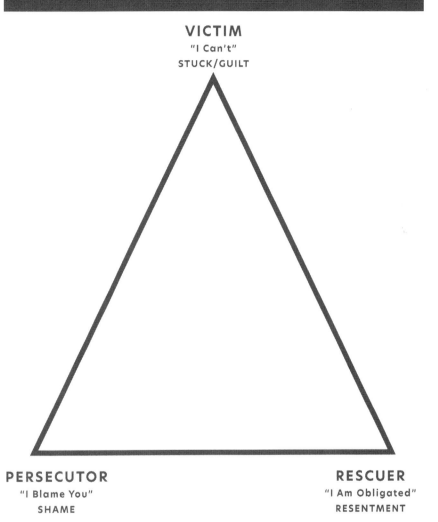

THE KARPMAN DRAMA TRIANGLE

VICTIM
"I Can't"
STUCK/GUILT

PERSECUTOR
"I Blame You"
SHAME

RESCUER
"I Am Obligated"
RESENTMENT

THE KARPMAN DRAMA TRIANGLE[17]

The drama triangle is a tool used in psychotherapy and specifically in an approach called transactional analysis, and it's a triangle of "actors in the drama," if you will, that highlights how as humans in relationships we are either a persecutor, a victim, or a rescuer.

The triangle shows that we tend to not only bounce between all three within ourselves, but we play out these particular dramas within the dynamics in all our relationships. When playing out the roles within the drama triangle, we give away our power, believing that we are beholden to persecution, to rescuing, or to victimhood.

HSE SHADOW TO STRENGTH PATHWAYS

	EMPATHY	INTUITION	CREATIVITY
Strength			
Empowerment	COACH	CHALLENGER	CREATOR
Drama	RESCUER	PERSECUTOR	VICTIM
Shadow	OVER-RESPONSIBILITY	OVER-PROTECTION	OVERWHELM

In our Shadow to Strength Pathways, you'll see the aspects of the drama triangle in the second row from the bottom . Now let's look at the row titled Empowerment, and the words that fall under Empowerment: Coach, Challenger, and Creator. These aspects make up another triangle called the Empowerment Dynamic Triangle, otherwise referred to as TED, The Empowerment Dynamic, or the TED Triangle. This triangle was developed by David Emerald, who is a master speaker, teacher, facilitator, and storyteller.[18] The TED Triangle was his creation to address the ways to escape from the dreaded drama triangle. TED inspires the realization that choice can lead to a positive approach to any of life's challenges, that when you find yourself in the drama triangle, there's actually an empowered way out.

Now, let's look at the bottom row of the Shadow to Strength Pathways, the shadow row: Over-Responsibility, Over-Protection, and Overwhelm. At the top is the Strength row: Empathy, Intuition, and Creativity. What we see here are the specific pathways from the shadow row up to the Strength row, and particularly how the drama triangle and the TED triangle relate specifically to us as highly sensitives. They show not only how we can bounce between the shadows of over-responsibility, over-protection, and overwhelm, but more importantly how to get out of them.

We recognize that when we are in over-responsibility, we are caught in the drama of "rescuing." But we see our way out, which is through the "coach" and our highly sensitive strength of empathy. The same goes for every single pathway from over-protection to intuition, from overwhelm to creativity: for each drama, the way out is through empowerment and our highly sensitive strengths. Now let's go back to fear versus intuition, and Dr. Siegel's representation of the brain. When we are in our shadows, or the drama, our lid is flipped.

We can use energy management to support us in accessing empowerment and our strengths so we can flip the switch. We can bring down the lid, accessing our amygdala *and* frontal cortex, which gives us access to creative solutions. Doing so allows us to empathize, put ourselves in someone else's shoes, and access our intuition as guidance and our strength of creativity.

What can be most powerful when working with the Shadow to Strength Pathways is that the shadows and the drama, rather than becoming triggers that lead us into behaviors of rescuing, persecuting, or feeling and being a victim, instead become signals or ways that we are touched and reminded: "Wait, there is another way." You have the power to access empowerment through the coach, the challenger, and the creator and to access your strengths of empathy, intuition, and creativity. You are not beholden to a life of highly sensitive shame, but rather you are emboldened to create your business, work, and your life as a highly sensitive leader.

Brianna's Story

In 2015, I found Heather and A Course in Business Miracles. At the time, my business, Sylver Consulting, an innovation consulting practice serving Fortune 1000 organizations and city governments, was growing and thriving; however, I was not. My business was running me. I wasn't enjoying my work, nor was I secure in my skills and capacity as a leader.

I knew the innovation work I was doing was what I was meant to do. But I also knew that if I was going to continue to do it—and rise to my full potential in it—I needed to do it differently. I did not know what that meant at that time. But that intuition led me to step into my first engagement with the Business Miracles program.

I was quickly introduced to the "highly sensitive" concept. One of the strengths that many highly sensitives have is being deeply spiritual. I had always considered myself to be spiritual; however, I believed in God from a theoretical head space. I did not lead my life with the energy of Jesus and God at the forefront of my actions. Business Miracles, despite its lack of religious affiliation, has personally given me the courage, energy, and tools to truly surrender to God.

One of the most powerful Business Miracles visioning tools for me is the *intuitive planning process*. This is a planning experience in which you meditatively access your heart, not your head, to understand where you are meant to go next in your business and life.

My very first time doing an intuitive plan, I received clear guidance from God that I am meant to rise as a spiritual leader in my industry. Now, I will tell you, I still have no idea what that really means. I was so uncomfortable with this message at first that I couldn't say the phrase "spiritual leader." I had to modify it to "practical spiritual leader" to even open myself up to the possibilities of what I was being called to do.

However, instead of dismissing this call as I might have done before, I started exploring it actively in daily auto-writing with God. And as next steps were shown to me, I took them. As a result, I have achieved some powerful milestones.

Back in 2017, I was asked to keynote an innovation conference at Notre Dame on the topic of Overcoming Innovation Anxiety. That talk was about acknowledging and naming the fears and anxieties that stop innovation in its tracks, and how to transform that fear and anxiety into a form of productive learning that promotes growth and love of self. That talk was received with great acclaim.

Since then, my organization has grown to be a partner with many Fortune 1000 organizations, supporting transformative and systemic business change. In 2019, through my adjunct faculty role with the IIT Institute of Design in Chicago, Illinois, I led a team of students in researching and writing a thought leadership report about how enterprises of all sizes can more intentionally Appropriate Design to lead with greater purpose in their respective industries. Appropriate Design is designing something suitable, meaningful, beautiful, and functional—something that works for many reasons. I have also personally coached more than thirty cities in how to co-create with their residents, including historically under-represented groups, to develop new programs and policies tackling big issues such as transit, climate change, homelessness, opioid substance abuse, and more.

With each action I take, I am helping others rise up to a better version of themselves and the organizations they represent. I'm showing people how to lead with light and curiosity versus fear and anxiety … something so needed in business today.

I still don't see the full vision that God has for my "spiritual leader" call. I know, with certainty, that there is more work to do. With faith, I take each step that is shown to me. With each action taken, I see with greater clarity my purpose. This supports me to walk my journey with joy and up-leveled intention versus the reaching and anxious energy that was abundant in my life before.

Business Miracles and The Highly Sensitive Leadership Training Program for Entrepreneurs have provided the framework for me to action God in my daily life and feel centered, grounded, and held. I am forever grateful for this support, which continues to take new shapes as I and the community evolve.

POWER OF YOUR MOST MAGNIFICENT SELF

As Brianna so powerfully shared, when we are operating from our highly sensitive strengths such as intuition in all parts of our work and life, especially areas not typically associated with utilizing these strengths, such as planning, everything requires less effort, aligning us to create more impact and then also more income. Rest is no longer associated with "recovery" as part of the coping cycle, but instead is associated with an intentional space of stillness and deep, internal connection that we consciously create by building this space into our day-to-day activities as an ongoing core practice.

We are able to release the grip of socialized comparison as well as the *myth of arrival*—recognizing that there is no magic destination or amount of income that will dissolve all our troubles—but instead owning who we are as highly sensitives and structuring all our work and life to honor our needs so we're able to operate from our strengths consistently. Highly sensitive leadership becomes an intentional journey of wash-rinse-rest-repeat. We are at peace.

The intuitive planning process I teach in the Highly Sensitive Leadership Training Program for Entrepreneurs is a key element that supports this type of ongoing, core practice approach, and it is also a full day process. But to begin, you can use the following activation as a daily entryway to your most magnificent self as a highly sensitive leader. I recommend that you read the passage below, Activation: Power of Your Most Magnificent Self, each day, make a recording of yourself reading it to listen to, or create art around it—or whatever form of daily expression will support you with making this connection. What's most important is that, whatever you do, you do so consistently.

ACTIVATION: POWER OF YOUR MOST MAGNIFICENT SELF

As a highly sensitive leader, I am literally coded to be successful. I am everything the world desperately needs right now. My time has come, and a miracle is a shift in perception, which is exactly what's required for highly sensitive leader success.

I prepare myself to receive. I give myself the gift of being here, being present, and to support that decision, I take in a strong, steady breath. I breathe in, and I let it out. And again, I breathe in and let it out. I feel myself fully coming into my body. I feel myself opening my mind. I feel myself connecting with my heart.

I take a strong, steady breath in, and I let it out.

In this moment, right here, right now, I begin to tap into my most magnificent self, my highest self. I tap into my magnificent self by answering this question: if I had no fear, where would I go and what would I do?

I let this answer come to me in this moment, right now.

Now I take it one step further. I ask myself, if I was able to release all the nitty-gritties of "the hows" before I took action, what would I be free to do and who would I be free to be?

I let the answer come to me in this moment right now: What would I be free to do? And who would I be free to be?

I simply take note. I might hear, see, or sense something specific, or it might simply be a feeling or maybe colors or random images. No right, no wrong, no judgment. I simply take note.

I take in a strong, steady breath, and I let it out.

I receive the gift that my inner guidance is giving to me now. I say to my inner self, "I hear you. I see you. I receive this. Whether it makes sense to me or not does not matter. I allow this energy, this message to be imprinted on my soul in this moment. I will hold it dear, and I know it will be there for me as a guide exactly when I need it in the exact ways that I need it, in the forms that I need it.

"I accept that and I receive that now."

Jessica's Story

"Start with a fierce commitment to consistent energy management," Heather said.

Standing at the front of the room, in a puddle of tears, I had just finished sharing with my mastermind group how I felt like my soul was being crushed by an invisible glass ceiling of income generation in my business ever since I had gotten married two years prior.

That glass ceiling was crushing my soul for three reasons:

1. Getting married had triggered a psychological safety net and a slide into old patterns of financial dependence rather than the financial independence I deeply desired.
2. My husband, Zach, had made it clear that he was ready to leave his cushy corporate job and become self-employed, so my psychological safety net would soon be gone.
3. The universe had bigger plans for me. It came through clearly on my intuitive plan just a day earlier that it was time to generate $25,000 a month consistently in my business—double what I had been making.

I had been reaching my base dire need income goals in my business consistently for years, and had generated a profitable, sustainable, and mid-six-figure business thanks to my work with Heather. I knew in my heart that it was time for me to step up and be willing to generate more than I ever had before, consistently. But my mind was a tornado of thoughts, spinning with wonder about *How?!* and *This is crazy!*

This is where most business coaches would unload an overwhelming marketing and launch strategy that would put my highly sensitive self into an early grave. But as I stood in front of the room and dried my tears, Heather responded with an approach I least expected.

She simply said, "Start with a fierce commitment to consistent energy management about what it would mean for you and your relationship to Zach for you to generate $25,000 a month consistently in your business. What energy management immediately comes to mind?"

"Auto-writing," I replied.

"Great," she said. "I recommend you stay committed to it daily for at least thirty days. The most important thing is that you're doing it when you don't want to."

Challenge accepted. Although, if I'm honest, I had *no* idea how writing in my journal every day would create double the income. But from working with Heather for years, I've learned to do my assignment and see what happens.

The next day, I dedicated a brand-new journal to my commitment to auto-writing. Calling in my higher powers, I wrote at the top of the page: "What would it mean for me and my relationship to Zach for me to generate $25,000 a month consistently in my business?" Each day, I'd share with Heather what came through this process by posting it on our Business Miracles Community forum.

Within the first five days of my thirty-day commitment, Heather acknowledged how powerful this process was going to be for me and recommended I do this auto-writing daily until the next training retreat, which was months away. Challenge accepted.

Over the next 135 days, including weekends, holidays, and even on Christmas, I found a quiet space to sit down, connect in, and ask. And each day, I was given guidance that left an imprint on my soul as I went about my normal day-to-day business. No major marketing changes or crazy overwhelming launches—I just stuck to my auto-writing. I never missed a day.

That first month that I started my auto-writing, I created $25,000 in receivable income in my business, double what I had done before. The second month, in came another $25,000. Then another $25,000 month. And another and another and another.

Each month I had a fierce commitment to auto-writing, I generated $25,000 in my business. Consistently.

Thanks to this process, when talks about my husband leaving his job would happen, instead of feeling frozen, anxious, and scared, I felt a deep sense of peace, calm, and confidence about it. This process was giving me such a sense of safety and trust. I was even excited for him! For us!

Midway through this energy management commitment, the pandemic of 2020 hit. But thanks to this process and being able to consistently generate $25,000 months, I was safe.

Looking back, I can see the income goal the universe gave me for my intuitive plan was about something much more than just the money. Through Heather's mentoring and my fierce commitment to this different approach, not only did I have a financial safety net during the pandemic, I had finally become my own psychological safety net.

LET GO TO LET IN

I once heard from a spiritual teacher somewhere along my journey, "Everyone wants transformation, but no one wants to change." This means true change requires you to look at the ways you've been behaving up until now that have not been so helpful or supportive, and it also requires you to let go of behaviors that have become very comfortable, just as Jessica shared. This brings us back to our very first question: will you accept the challenge?

Shifting from experiencing your highly sensitive nature as a weakness, a hindrance, or from a place of being a victim to an experience of strength, privilege, and empowerment, like any chosen change, is a process. It's one that is much easier when it is not done alone. Find others like you who are invested in an empowerment journey to travel the path with you. It might be about getting in touch with me and my team to find out if the Highly Sensitive Leadership Training Program for Entrepreneurs is for you, or finding a local support group, or starting your own. Whatever it might be, transformation is easier when in community and in like-minded connection rather than isolation. Find what works for you, but find something.

For many years, I had difficulty determining if a group was right for me or not and would often find myself either having the repeated experience of feeling like the odd one out (that 20 percent again) or being called on to lead the group even when I just wanted to be a participant. And as I mentored more and more highly sensitives, I found I was not the only one; this was a shared experience for many of us.

This is why we've created clear guidelines and structures within our programs to ensure it is an inclusive, supportive learning environment, using what we refer to as the guiding principles of highly sensitive leadership. These principles can act almost like a checklist for yourself. First, you can use them to see if the deeper work we do in our programs might be a match for you, but you can also use them to help find another support group to be involved in, or even with overall decision-making, asking yourself, "Will this help me let go and let in?"

LET GO TO LET IN	
LET GO	**LET IN**
Analysis-Paralysis	Intuitive Discernment and Decision-Making
Taking Things Personally	Personal Responsibility
Trigger-Driven Reactions	Triggers as Awakenings/ Learnings
Avoiding Conflict	Courageous/Difficult Conversations
Over-Protecting Your Energy	Discomfort Resilience
Resistance	Grace and Grit
Needing to Be Liked By Everyone	Conscientiously Speaking Up
Operating from Limiting Beliefs	Consistent Assessment
People Pleasing	Empathetic Awareness
Trying to Do It All Alone	Collaborative Creation
Perfectionism	Flexibility and Fluidity
Conforming to the Other 80 Percent	Daring to Do Things Differently
Comparison	Celebrating Baby Steps
Driven by FEAR	Guided by TRUST

CHOICE POINT ... AGAIN

As highly sensitive leaders, we have a choice to make. As we move forward into our post-pandemic "new world," we want to consistently be checking in and facing that choice point on the Resistance to Resilience chart, asking these questions: Am I going to stay in anxiety? Am I going to stay in my shadows? Am I going to stay in my coping mechanism? Am I going to stay in resistance?

Or am I going to choose grace and grit? Am I going to call on community? Am I going to call on core practices? Am I going to call on consistency, and am I going to choose to stay in the upper half of the comparison chart as an act of resilience?

To be able to do this, you need to know who you are—not who someone else expects you to be, not who you've made yourself into for someone else, and not who you feel like you have to be to create business, career, or life success. You must know who you are. And then you must know how you're here to serve, and who you are here to serve, and make all decisions from this place.

Use this book as your guide, and go forward to lead as the highly sensitive that you are. I have full faith in you.

ABOUT THE
CONTRIBUTORS

Lorna Lange is a business coach and community curator for highly sensitive leadership training programs at A Course in Business Miracles. She also works with individuals looking for more energy, ease, and joy through applying the transformational inner practices and teachings of yoga.

Lidia Bonilla is a pleasure strategist whose work has been featured in the *New York Times*, *Forbes*, and *Essence* magazine. She helps organizations and individuals heal from burnout by redefining productivity through pleasure. She is the co-founder and advisor of the Women of Sex Tech, a global organization dedicated to merging sex and technology. www.lidiabonilla.com

Melissa Patterson is an actor and intuitive reader making her way in New York City. www.melissaapatterson.com

Stephanie Bonte-Lebair is a professional singer turned voice, presentation, and sales coach. She performed in New York City and beyond before creating her business, The Empowered Voice. She helps singers, speakers, and business professionals leverage their voices for more influence. Her website is www. empoweryourvoice.com.

Kara-Lee Golota is the creator of www.LoveThruNature. com. She continues to be guided by the Holy Horse Spirits through her herd of five equines. Her work inspires and empowers others with financial-gardening and deep experiences of connection through horses and nature.

Dr. Chandy Lopes is a naturopathic doctor and the owner of Renew Wellness. She specializes in hormone replacement and balancing for men and women, IV nutritional therapy, and helping her patients feel better to live better lives. Her website is www. RenewWellness.Life.

Melissa E. Anders uses her highly sensitive strengths that make her a natural writing and life coach to serve and support academics and academic professionals who have a desire to take personal responsibility and do academia differently by moving away from old "sink or swim" approaches of academic culture to innovative approaches of being supported and transforming through their work together. Her website is www.melissaeanders.com.

Brian Murphy is a graduate of Trinity College Dublin. He has worked as a primary school teacher and educator for twenty years. He now specializes in teaching children and adults about the principles of healthy breathing. His breathing programs can be accessed at his website www.yourbreath.ie.

Macy Askari-Robinson is following her intuition to transition out of her business as a brow and permanent cosmetic artist to fulfill her purpose as an energy and mindfulness coach.

Geri Deane is passionate about her role as a REALTOR®. Whether her clients are buying, selling, or renting a home, or looking for relocation assistance, her goal is to exceed expectations as her clients make life's most important lifestyle and investment decisions. www.gerideane.com

Ennis Carter is the founding director of Social Impact Studios. Ennis specializes in engaging people in critical issues and culture through artistry and activism. Her websites are socialimpactstudios.com and enniscarter.com.

Gabrielle Fauste is a teacher and consultant who specializes in evidence-informed, innovative interventions to support the development and agency of her students and clients as change-makers in the responsible tech movement.

Khayra Bundakji of khayrab.com serves professionals, solopreneurs, and entrepreneurs in promoting themselves from a place of inner peace. Using online courses, workshops, and her personal branding program, her clients receive clarity on who their dream audiences are, what to say, and how to say it *naturally*.

Jessica Procini is the founder and leader of Escape From Emotional Eating. Since 2011, she has been helping women on a mission heal the roots of their emotional eating so they can embody their full potential. Learn more about her life-changing work at EscapeFromEmotionalEating.com.

Brianna Sylver leads Sylver Consulting, an international innovation research and strategy firm supporting Fortune 1000 organizations to courageously embrace change and future-proof their offerings. Sylver supports organizations to strengthen their brands, fill their innovation pipelines, and align stakeholders around new visions for growth. Her website is http://www.sylverconsulting.com.

ABOUT HEATHER DOMINICK

AFTER A SELF-EMPLOYMENT "dark night of the soul," Heather Dominick changed everything about how she went about being in business, from marketing, to selling, and especially day-to-day operations. These changes led to such a positive shift in her level of happiness while allowing her to continue to generate a solid, sustainable income, she knew she had to share her experience with others.

Heather is a graduate of NYU, where she received her first coach training. As a high school drama teacher, she had the privilege of participating in an innovative NYC public school business partnership program, which included intimately collaborating on curriculum, stage, and costume design with none other than Bette Midler.

Heather is the winner of the 2015 Best of Manhattan Coaching Award and creator of the 2014 Stevie Award-winning virtual event, *A Course In*

Business Miracles: 21-Day Discovery Series, which attracted close to 6,000 registrants from countries and continents around the world including Iceland, Nigeria, Russia, Asia, South America, Australia, Europe, and the US.

Heather has appeared on *Lifetime* television, and has been published in numerous books, including *Stepping Stones to Success* alongside Deepak Chopra.

Heather teaches

- how to cultivate your highly sensitive strengths;
- how to make more impact and income by operating from this unique set of strengths;
- how these strengths position you to lead;
- why highly sensitive leadership is important now more than ever.

An exceptional facilitator and teacher, Heather is known for creating a safe, sacred environment for true transformation, whether delivering training online or in-person. Since 2010, Heather has taught thousands of highly sensitive entrepreneurs and leaders from around the globe how to release lifelong limiting beliefs, overcome fears, and develop new leadership skills to excel in business and life. By doing things differently, we can all create more impact and more income with a lot less effort.

Heather lives and thrives in the heart of New York City with her sweetheart husband, Stephen. Visit www.businessmiracles.com or email info@businessmiracles.com for more information about Heather's work.

ACKNOWLEDGMENTS

CLEARLY THIS BOOK WAS MEANT to be created in collaboration. I am so grateful for all the energy that was contributed to bringing this project to fruition. I would like to acknowledge:

- Alexandra of Your Resident Wordsmith, Richard of My Word Publishing, and Victoria of Wolf Design and Marketing. Thank you for "getting me," honoring the work, and not trying to make it into something it isn't. This is priceless to a highly sensitive person.
- All past, present, and future members of the Business Miracles Team who have supported the forward movement of this sacred mission in one way or another.
- A particular acknowledgment to the team members who directly contributed to "the book": Suzie Mitchell, Heather Sluss, Joelle Lydon.
- An even more particular acknowledgment to team member Lorna

Lange. I am beyond grateful and in continuous awe of our sacred contract, our years together, and to have found someone who values continuous growth as much as I do. I can't even write these words without tearing up.

+ All my past, present, and future students, including those from days as a traditional classroom teacher at Hewlett High School and Washington Irving High School, as I've learned so much from each of you, and especially every student in the Business Miracles Community. Everything I create is to support you on your journey of empowerment as a highly sensitive entrepreneur and leader.

+ Too many friends and colleagues to name who have been influential. If we've shared a deep conversation or a mastermind discussion, I am grateful.

+ Rosemarie Bray and Leslie Zema: our going on twenty-year commitment to "Good Happenings" and staying connected when I chose to step away from The Performing Arts House have been invaluable to me.

+ Shira Epstein: we've traveled far and wide since our days at NYU over many "seasons." You are one of the most intuitively intelligent people I know, and I am beyond grateful for both your friendship and highly sensitive leadership every day. Here's to another twenty-five-plus years.

+ My parents, Dennis and Nanci Dominick: without you, there would be no me. I am grateful for all of it.

+ My grandmother, Christine Dominick, who I'm pretty sure was highly sensitive, and was always my quiet, loving refuge and my first model of morning energy management.

+ My sweetheart husband, Stephen, my most important person, my love, my everything. You said to me when we first met that you were committed to the growth of our relationship and to "stay together." You've proven this time and time again, and each time my abandoned heart has been given room to heal one stitch more. Thank you for loving this "chipmunk" with your "bear" heart. Anything and everything I've been able to create over the past twenty years is because of your support.

ABOUT THE BUSINESS MIRACLES COMMUNITY

Are you ready to ...

+ make more income?
+ create more impact?
+ experience more ease?

At A Course in Business Miracles, we facilitate twelve-month programs dedicated to your transformation and retraining from shadows to strengths.

WHAT DOES IT MEAN TO BE A *HIGHLY SENSITIVE ENTREPRENEUR?*

Being highly sensitive is how you were born into the world. **Your nervous system is literally wired differently,** and as a result you take in stimulation at a much higher degree, whether that be sight, sound, smell, touch, energy, or information.

How do you learn to be in charge of yourself and your purpose? **You do this by retraining your nervous system.**

In our Highly Sensitive Leadership Training Programs for Entrepreneurs, you…

…gain a new level of ability to focus, allowing you to create more in less time with a lot more joy.

…create marketing that makes you money without trying to be someone you're not.

…gain increased respect within all your relationships, including prospects, clients, and team.

WE ARE A GLOBAL, INCLUSIVE COMMUNITY.

This training program is inclusive and supportive of all nations, religions, and races. We are a global community dedicated to effecting positive change and increased prosperity for all, equally.

Our mission is to help you do things differently without sacrificing your own needs so you can make more of an impact and income in the world.

Learn more and join us at:
www.businessmiracles.com

ENDNOTES

1   Elaine N. Aron, *The Highly Sensitive Person: How to Thrive When The World Overwhelms You* (New York: Citadel Press, 2020), 13.

2   Aron, *The Highly Sensitive Person*, 17.

3   Sharon Wilson, "Coaching From Spirit." accessed June 6, 2022, https://coachingfromspiritinstitute.com/.

4   DARE to do. Motivation, "The Story of the Golden Buddha (life changing)," December 2, 2020, YouTube video, 2:36, https://www.youtube.com/watch?v=Cgb2SDjydCc.

5   For more on shame, see Linda M. Hartling et al., "Shame and Humiliation: From Isolation to Relational Transformation," *Work in Progress*, no. 88 (2000), Wellesley Centers for Women, Wellesley College, https://www.humiliationstudies.org/documents/hartling/HartlingShameHumiliation.pdf; Linda M. Hartling, bio, Wellesley Centers for Women, Wellesley College, accessed June 7, 2022 https://www.wcwonline.org/Inactive-Researchers/linda-m-hartling-phd.

6   FtMyersFamPsych, "Dr. Daniel Siegel presenting a Hand Model of the Brain," accessed February 29, 2021, YouTube video, 2:31, https://www.youtube.com/watch?v=gm9CIJ74Oxw; Building Better Brains, "Our Reaction to Stress Explained: How to use 'The Hand Model of the Brain,'" accessed December 24, 2019, https://buildingbetterbrains.com.au/hand-model-of-the-brain/; TEDx Talks, "Mindfulness and Neural Integration: Daniel Siegel, MD, at TEDxStudioCityED," accessed May 2, 2012, YouTube video, 18:26, https://www.youtube.com/watch?v=LiyaSr5aeho.

7   Martha Nibley Beck, *Finding Your Own North Star: Claiming the Life You Were Meant to Live* (New York: Three Rivers Press, 2001), 4.

8   Tara Brach, "The Power of Radical Acceptance: Healing Trauma through the Integration of Buddhist Meditation and Psychotherapy," accessed November 29, 2021, https://www.tarabrach.com/articles-interviews/trauma/.

9   APA Dictionary of Psychology, "Trauma," American Psychiatric Association, https://dictionary.apa.org/trauma, accessed June 28, 2022.

10   Mental Health Center of San Diego, "What are the 3 types of trauma?" March 8, 2021, https://mhcsandiego.com/what-are-the-3-types-of-trauma.

11   Davidson Scales, "Davidson Scales for Anxiety, PTSD, and Resilience," accessed November 10, 2021, https://www.davidsonscales.com/davidson-trauma-scale; American Psychological Association, *Clinical Practice Guideline for the Treatment of Posttraumatic Stress Disorder*, "PTSD Assessment Instruments," accessed November 10, 2021, https://www.apa.org/ptsd-guideline/assessment.

12 Meggan Watterson, *Mary Magdalene Revealed: The First Apostle, Her Feminist Gospel & the Christianity We Haven't Tried Yet* (New York City: Hay House, Inc., 2012), 95.

13 *A Course In Miracles*, Chapter 15, Section III, "Littleness versus Magnitude," accessed October 11, 2021, https://acim.org/acim/chapter-15/littleness-versus-magnitude/en/s/192.

14 D.W. Winnicott, *Playing and Reality* (London and New York: Taylor & Francis, 2012), 13-14.

15 Avram Alpert, "The Good Enough Life," *The NY Times*, February 20, 2019, https://www.nytimes.com/2019/02/20/opinion/the-good-enough-life-philosophy.html.

16 Stephen B. Karpman, "The New Drama Triangles," USATAA/ITAA conference lecture August 11, 2007, Free Download Worksheet for the DVD, https://karpmandramatriangle.com/pdf/thenewdramatriangles.pdf.

17 Adapted to show the Victim at the top, rather than bottom.

18 Center for The Empowerment Dynamic, "TED* (*The Empowerment Dynamic)," accessed November 10, 2021, https://powerofted.com/empowerment-triangle/.

Made in the USA
Middletown, DE
04 April 2023

27926319R00084